PAULA'S STORY

Chicken Shed would like to thank their friend Jonathan Shalit for his encouragement and help in securing publication of this book.

PAULA'S STORY

Shirley Flack

Foreword by Diana, Princess of Wales

With an introduction by Jo Collins and
Mary Ward, MBE, co-founders of the
Chicken Shed Theatre Company

HEADLINE

First published in 1997
by HEADLINE BOOK PUBLISHING

10 9 8 7 6 5 4 3 2 1

British Library Cataloguing in Publication Data

Flack, Shirley
  Paula's story
  1.Rees, Paula
  2.Cerebral palsied - Great Britain - Biography
  3.Lyricists - Great Britain - Biography
  I.Title
  616.8'36'0092

ISBN 0 7472 1772 6

Typeset by
Letterpart Limited, Reigate, Surrey

Printed and bound in Great Britain by
Mackays of Chatham PLC, Chatham, Kent

HEADLINE BOOK PUBLISHING
A division of Hodder Headline PLC
338 Euston Road
London NW1 3BH

'The most extraordinary experiences in the theatre involve the audience's social conscience as well as its deep emotional recognition. I had one of those rare experiences when I saw the Chicken Shed Theatre Company for the first time. The idea of the company shows us a glimpse of a more perfect world in which human beings of every kind share their talents in mutual dependence. Their work demands both our attention and our support.'

Trevor Nunn, director designate of the Royal National Theatre and a Chicken Shed trustee

CONTENTS

There is a saying "If a child lives with encouragement, he learns confidence. If a child lives with acceptance and friendship he learns to give love to the world".

It is these essential qualities of life that I associate with Chicken Shed and which it brings to all young people who tread its boards.

As with all Chicken Shed's young protégés, Paula Rees epitomises what that encouragement, acceptance and friendship means in terms of transforming a life and her devoted parents have every reason to be proud of the achievements which Chicken Shed has enabled her to attain.

When I became Patron of Chicken Shed in 1989, it was the beginning for me of a very happy relationship, experiencing at first hand the wealth of enthusiasm, talent and dedication generated by Mary Ward and Jo Collins, together with their remarkable team.

As a mother myself, I can identify with the fulfilment which Chicken Shed brings to so many families; as a lover of art I derive great pleasure at their contribution to theatre. Mary and Jo strive for excellence and as the young people they inspire know, it is so much easier when everyone says you can, rather than you can't!

Diana

October, 1996

INTRODUCTION

Being part of Paula's story has been a privilege, not just knowing Paula, but knowing Jan and Eddie, Kerri and Ian and Adam, because they are incredible people. Jan, for instance, given another environment in which to grow up would have achieved so much through her massive intelligence and dynamism. As it is she has used her considerable strengths to fight the battle for Paula, a battle which has, frankly, worn her out, so it is good now to see that she has begun to indulge herself, to enjoy her caravan for instance, to allow others to help in many ways.

Paula once wrote: 'You unfold my life.' That was a huge compliment. She has caused all our lives to unfold, and not just us, her family too; their lives are quite different because of Paula's unfolding life.

We have been lucky to have the opportunity to tell Paula's story. There are of course other stories we would like to tell, and then there are our own individual stories.

Mary: There's my own story which involves my parents, my Aunt Helen and all my friends who were part of my formative years; Manus and his family and friends, and my beautiful sons from whom I have learned so much, and the people who sustain me through the many struggles which present themselves daily and keep me believing and understanding.

Jo: My story is in many ways similar to Mary's. I too have my family and friends to acknowledge and thank for their support and encouragement. My story contains my music which has been part of my life always, which flows like a river, certain words bringing an unquestionable melody, they join and continue to flow. It is totally fulfilling.

There is the 'Jo and Mary' story, our very special relationship and the fact that it is out of that relationship that Chicken Shed has come. Jo has said she had found a soulmate. Soulmate is a common expression but a lot of people who use it don't believe in souls. We do, and we are indeed soulmates. There is a deep spiritual dimension to our relationship.

Then there is Chicken Shed itself, its development, the Chicken Shed story before Paula got involved. Paula has affected it hugely, and so have a lot of other people affected it hugely, and they will continue to do so. Each of them has a story, all of them important and some of them are extraordinary.

Recently a Chicken Shed mother wrote about the end-of-term performance here. From the audience, she watched her son Kip (who attends special school): 'The only child with his back to the audience, the only child performing as in a time lapse, the only child not in full costume. But as I watched, Kip gained in confidence, and his enjoyment started to sparkle. He missed his cue for his one spoken line . . . belatedly and unselfconsciously joining in . . . he so clumsily executed his dance steps, his tuneless voice joined loudly in song. Tears of pride streamed down my face, pride at my brave, lion-hearted son, at how far he had come in eight short years, pride as he put his all into joining in.

'For this is what Chicken Shed is all about, and that is what life is all about: joining in. So often that is what is denied Kip. Society forces him, and us, to live always on the edge. Rarely does it encourage or invite us. Like most people with disabilities, Kip is forced to live apart from the mainstream of life. Yet here he was, at Chicken Shed, proving that he may be disabled, but it is society that handicaps him. Remove those handicaps and he can perform with the rest, work, play and live with the rest.

'The performance ended. In the car travelling home, Kip's sister Matti was very quiet. Finally she said: "Why can't Kip's whole life be like his Chicken Shed life?" Oh from the mouths of ten-year-olds! Why not indeed?'

Our objective is somehow to bring about that change, so that every child's life is like their Chicken Shed life. And their Chicken Shed life is based on value, individual worth; it is based on positives, on believing in people.

There are two main issues. One is the Chicken Shed philosophy, a way of working, a method. Then there is Chicken Shed itself. They are two separate strands. What we want is the Chicken Shed work to be taken on by everyone. It's for mainstream society to take on the Chicken Shed method and develop it, so that in years to come there will be a dancer who happens to have Down's syndrome, who doesn't know anything about Chicken Shed, but who goes to the local dancing school in, say, Lincoln because he wants to dance, and he develops into a great dancer and joins the Royal Ballet.

In the 1960s there was an American high jumper called Dick Fosbury. His style was to turn before jumping and flop onto his back. This was not the normally accepted routine – the world champion high jumper at that time, Valeriy Brumel, jumped conventionally, which was to go over the bar and land on his stomach. Once Dick Fosbury became world high jump champion and world record-holder, everybody accepted the 'Fosbury Flop'; and now if you watch any high jumping you'll find people using various methods to achieve their objective, the Fosbury Flop among them. But until he became the best in the world, no one believed it would work.

That's the position we're in at the moment. We have the burden of the proof of the method, and our work is judged by the method and the method is judged by our work.

Since we moved into our own theatre, the development and standard of the work has risen remarkably in every way, performance and direction almost reaching the level of the music which has always been way ahead. We've trained marvellous performers from nothing, we've had no help, no good facilities, no one to turn to. All we've had is disbelief.

With *A Midsummer Night's Dream*, we received

the best compliments we've ever had. People talked about how the production took theatre into another dimension. They didn't say it took caring into another dimension, or a social service into another dimension. And that is what we have been fighting for, to show our 'theatre'; to show that everyone has a contribution to make – to what they want to do. Our point is not that all children with Down's syndrome should be part of the theatre (not everyone wants to be part of the theatre), but that Down's syndrome has got nothing whatsoever to do with the person; it's a genetic thing which causes certain physical signs, it tells you nothing about the person. You want to do whatever it is because you're you. Our assertion is that if people want to take part in the theatre, not only should they be able to but the theatre should be grateful, and learn from them and take from them.

It's exciting working with people who are there because they have a natural love of being on stage, every one at a different level. Some have an almost scary facility for communicating with an audience, others have an ordinary, simple approach to it. It's a privilege for us to work in this way and to achieve results. It is a long and painful process because the whole time we are working, society is working against us.

One of the most positive factors in at last having our own building is that people now have somewhere to be, safely, to show their emotions and show their talent, where people believe in them. People ask why don't people leave. Why would they leave when it is part of their life? It belongs to them, it *is* them.

The financial implications of our development have been frightening. It takes a lot of money to run our organisation. When balanced with what we are achieving it is a small price to pay. How do you attach a sum of money to life, to self-worth, to people's own aspirations? But the reality is we have no money, we struggle to survive.

The future is the bit we worry about. We do need to develop people to guarantee the future and we are trying to do that, quickly, so that we can relax and know there will always be a Chicken Shed. Over the past few years Jo has trained and encouraged others to compose music with some conspicuous successes. There are now several excellent writers of music within Chicken Shed; the more confident they become and the more of them who emerge, the more comfortable we will be about the future.

Receiving the MBE was an honour for which Mary is proud and thankful, but it is not an individual award. It is for Jo and John, and belongs to everyone who has contributed over the years and especially to those who still work so hard on a daily basis to make Chicken Shed what it is. It is for 'services to the arts', which we all hope signifies a change in attitude and an acknowledgement of Chicken Shed's contribution to the theatre by those with influence in the arts and those who distribute arts funding.

We both have a deep love for Paula, a special closeness and desire to go on developing with her.

Paula played Titania in *A Midsummer Night's Dream*, or one of three Titanias, reclining on 'the bank whereon the wild thyme blows', behind a gauze, like a dream in which you know what is there but you haven't got the detail, you have to look carefully, to use your imagination. Perhaps people will be able to see through the 'gauze' of *Paula's Story* to the other stories beyond. Hopefully by reading her story people will want to know more, to ask questions, to think about those other people whose stories are not known, to wonder about them and their lives. And ideally apply themselves to the story, and change their attitudes and their lives.

Jo Collins, Musical Director
Mary Ward, MBE, Artistic Director
Co-founders of the Chicken Shed Theatre Company

PREFACE

The date is 23 April 1994. The place, the Criterion Theatre at Piccadilly Circus. Every seat is taken. There are faces in the auditorium that usually belong the other side of the footlights. This is a celebrity audience. On stage, four young actors, a singer-pianist and a dark-haired girl with shining eyes seated beside the piano, her pale face luminous. She does not speak, yet she is the star of *Paula: The Story So Far*. The star, the lyricist, the inspiration.

In a box is her mother, Jan Rees, watching as the play is received with tears and tumultuous applause. As one reviewer is to describe it: 'If the West End of London has hosted a more remarkable production, it can hardly have staged one that has beaten such miraculous odds to arrive there, or one with a more moving and uplifting message about the indefatigability of the human spirit.'

Later, after the hugs from strangers, the kisses, the congratulations, Jan cries. It is a relief, crying for Paula, crying for Eddie and the family, crying for herself. The family goes home. Eddie, who has been helping backstage, carries Paula from the

Number One dressing room, and she leaves the theatre as she arrived, via the lift to the ground floor goods entrance, in her wheelchair.

CHAPTER 1

I wish I could talk

I wish I could walk
I wish I could talk
I wish I was like everyone else

I wish I had a failure
I wish I had a success
I wish I did not care so much
I wish I did not care

I see sadness
I see pain
I see love, hope and kindness

I see a good life
And so do you if you try
So let time do its work
And we will all be loved

Jan Bentley was not quite fifteen when Eddie Rees first saw her, a young blonde girl with her mother at her side being shown around the factory where he worked as a cutter. Three weeks later she joined the firm, the Jane Shilton handbag factory in London's East End. Although Eddie was officially courting someone else at the time, he soon transferred his affections to Jan and they started going out.

Eddie, then nineteen, lived with his parents in Dagenham, Essex; Jan's home was Enfield in north London – the same house where they live today. He wasn't her first boyfriend but the first she regarded as 'serious', and in the style of the times they eventually got engaged, saved up, and were married, after a five-year courtship, on 11 June 1966 at St Andrew's Church in Enfield.

Jan and Eddie started married life on £12 a week combined wages, and moved into two rooms of a three-bedroom house in St Mary's Road, Edmonton, rent one guinea a week. To avoid having to share the kitchen, their amiable landlords, Mr and Mrs Campbell, agreed to let them instal a cooker in one of the rooms. They all got on happily together. But within months Jan was pregnant, and the need for more room was imminent.

The Campbells entreated them to stay, even offering the third bedroom; but the promise of a council flat won, and with tears on both sides they parted, moving to the poetically named Sir Lancelot House in Edmonton. The reality was not quite as poetic. Jan and Eddie's new flat was on the nineteenth floor, and high winds caused the entire building to sway perilously, or so it seemed. When it thundered, Jan had to be taken home to her mother's house until the storm had passed.

Soon after the birth of their daughter Kerri on 10 May 1967, they exchanged flats with another council tenant, moving to prettier surroundings nearby. This time the flat was on the sixth floor – a step in the right direction, they agreed.

Jan gave up work at the factory to stay home and look after the baby. They considered themselves very fortunate, and were happy and contented despite having very little money. Once Eddie had moved to working on the docks, with its bonus and piece rate schemes, their financial situation improved. When the budget stretched to an evening out – usually spent with Eddie's parents Helen and Charles at Charles's working men's club in Greenwich – Jan's mother Hilda and father Roy would oblige with the babysitting.

Paula was born in 1970. As with the first pregnancy, Jan felt nauseated throughout and vomited copiously. This time the doctor prescribed pills which alleviated the sickness, and on 5 January Jan went into labour and Eddie took her to hospital. It was to be a traumatic experience.

By evening, the midwife in charge asked Eddie to leave because, she said, nothing was happening nor would for many hours, and Jan was left alone in the delivery room. The midwife's prediction proved wrong, and her labour intensified.

She has wondered since if perhaps the midwife was deaf. Jan made enough noise and rang the bell but nobody came. So it was some considerable time before the midwife looked in to check, and by that time Jan was so advanced in labour that she was actually pushing. 'Of course you aren't,' said the midwife and bustled off. Jan said to herself that the midwife must know best, but at the same time common sense told her: 'You've had one baby and you know what bearing down means.'

She had delivered the baby's head and shoulders by the time the midwife next popped her head around the door, and amid a flurry of activity the medical staff assisted with the final part of the delivery. And Paula came into the room at 2 am on 6 January.

'I reached out to hold her, a fat podgy beautiful baby girl, seven pounds six ounces, with huge dark eyes and masses of thick black hair. She was perfect.'

Eddie had always said all he wanted was two daughters, so now their family was complete. They were euphoric. But before Jan and the baby went home, there was one small incident, a signal which, although disregarded at the time, was not forgotten.

In the maternity ward it was routine, before mother and baby were discharged, for the nurse to demonstrate the correct way of bathing the baby. As the nurse attempted to part Paula's legs to put on a clean nappy, she said: 'You're very awkward . . . you won't let me put your nappy on.' She seemed surprised to meet such resistance, such tightly clenched legs. Jan later learned that this was one of the signs of cerebral palsy.

Mother and baby went home, and Paula cried all day and all night. Because Jan had been unsuccessful at breastfeeding Kerri, she didn't attempt it with this second baby and persevered instead with the bottle. But Paula threw up her feed continuously. By the time she was a month old, she would gag on the bottle as soon as it touched her mouth. Eventually Jan cut a hole in the teat and tried to pour some milk into the baby's mouth that way; clearly she couldn't suck.

The clinic did not seem concerned about the baby's failure to gain weight, but there were other, equally disturbing symptoms. The baby would stiffen in her arms, as if in acute pain; jump convulsively at a sudden noise; and hardly ever opened her eyes, or rolled and flickered them about when she did. The family GP made reassuring noises – 'Don't worry, it's colic, it will all sort itself out' – which Jan would have liked to believe. But she had been through colic with Kerri, and colic had a pattern, a routine. This was all day, nonstop. This was different.

There was no one to turn to. Her GP treated her

as if she were the classic neurotic mother, even saying as much to another member of staff at the medical centre. Jan heard it on the grapevine and didn't doubt that he had said it for a moment. She was very worried. She didn't want to burden her mother with her fears, and Eddie, in the kindest way, didn't want to know. 'You're worrying about nothing,' he would say. 'It will all sort itself out.' So many people used those words that Jan began to think that perhaps they were right, that Paula was just one of those 'awkward' babies and that she must be patient, let things develop naturally. And wait.

Kerri was almost three by this time, so Jan's hands were full with caring for the two children. Her mother – a 'brilliant' support but working full time – was more than willing to babysit to give Jan and Eddie a break. But with Paula crying all the time, and Hilda and Roy having to be up very early for work, it became too much to ask. They were on their own.

Paula was seven months old when Jan, on yet another visit to the clinic, was seen by a new doctor on duty.

As the doctor began her examination, Jan started to tell her that she suspected there was something seriously wrong with Paula. She watched the doctor's face closely for some clue. Eventually the doctor spoke: 'I think she could be blind.'

Blind! That had never occurred to Jan. In a daze she heard the doctor say that an appointment would be made with the hospital paediatrician.

7

She told Eddie. The health visitor dropped by with a letter to take to the hospital, and Jan steamed it open. Blind: there it was in black and white. Curiously, it was almost a relief to have this explanation. You could do something about blindness, get advice, get treatment.

They had arranged to have a caravan holiday on the Isle of Wight. Jan, now seriously considering the possibility that Paula was blind, watched her closely, monitoring her responses to changes in light and movement. Paula's eyes rolled most of the time, she didn't like the light, was distressed by sunlight; but at night, when they walked from the caravan site into Sandown, she appeared to enjoy the sparkling street lights and illuminated signs in shops. This didn't seem to add up to blindness.

Appointment day arrived and they presented themselves at the hospital. During the lengthy examination, with Kerri silent, Jan talked about Paula's crying, not opening her eyes, the spasms, refusing to eat, recoiling if the wind touched her face or at the sound of a cough or a closing door. How she didn't do the usual baby things – smiling, gurgling, trying to sit up. The paediatrician listened. Then said: 'We'll let you know the results of our tests. Come back in three months.'

This time Jan was not prepared to wait. After a few weeks, armed with a purseful of small change for the telephone box on the corner, she rang the hospital, prepared to stay on the line as long as it took to find the right person in the right department to organise being seen at once. 'I can't wait any longer, I need to know,' she said, surprising herself at her own cheek. In Jan's culture, the doctor was close to God.

Her appointment was brought forward. The same doctor who had conducted the examination delivered her diagnosis. 'Cerebral palsy,' she said. 'She is microcephalic, quadriplegic and athetoid.'

What did this mean?

'It means she has severe brain damage.'

An image of collecting boxes outside shops, showing a child wearing calipers or sitting in a wheelchair. 'You mean she's a spastic?' entreated Jan. 'Like those children on the collecting boxes? Is she blind? Is she going to die?'

The facts were spelled out. Quadriplegia means paralysis of all four limbs and possibly the trunk. Athetosis is a disorder of the nervous system causing involuntary and uncontrollable movements. Microcephalia means very small brain. Microcephalic children are not expected to live beyond their teens, and are the most severely retarded of all.

At last Jan and Eddie knew for sure, and had a name for Paula's illness. It was even a relief to know what was wrong with her: now all Jan had to do was cope. The doctor said that the crying was to be expected. She knew what dealing with disability was like, and she understood. She proved to be very thoughtful, and would always come to the phone if Jan called with a problem. And, if Jan had to take Paula to Casualty, as often happened, the doctor would ensure she was seen at once on the ward instead.

9

The doctor offered no hope, however. There was no long-term prognosis, no cure. It was only when Jan said, 'There must be something I can do for Paula,' that the doctor spoke of physiotherapy, but this meant attending Harperbury Mental Hospital in St Albans, fifteen miles away.

'Yes, we'll do that,' said Jan, thinking that with physiotherapy, perhaps Paula would learn to walk.

Eddie and Jan didn't talk much about the diagnosis. 'She'll be all right. She's just slow, she'll catch up,' said Eddie, as he had been saying all along. It was to be a year before he could accept the truth. Jan didn't argue: it hurt too much to talk about it, and she kept her feelings to herself.

Soon afterwards Jan reported to the physiotherapy department at Harperbury, with Paula and Kerri in tow. They found the hospital to be a vast building, with blocks sprawling in all directions. The department was run by Professor Karel Bobath, a psychiatrist, and his wife Berta, a physiotherapist. Together they had formulated an innovative approach to the treatment of children with cerebral palsy, aiming through specialised techniques of handling to give affected children a greater variety of co-ordinated movement patterns.

In the physiotherapy room, children and babies lay on mats around the floor, while white-coated physiotherapists worked with other children on tables and chairs. It was here that, flanked by a small posse of students, first Professor Bobath, then Mrs Bobath, examined Paula gently and expertly. Then, holding her up for the students to observe,

Professor Bobath said: 'Here we have a nine-month baby with cerebral palsy. She is microcephalic, quadriplegic and athetoid. Note the small circumference of her head – she cannot hold her head up – and the way her leg rotates the wrong way. She suffers spasms.'

Turning to Jan, he said: 'Your baby is going to be very difficult to look after. My advice to you would be to have her placed in an institution, she would be better left here.'

Jan, shocked, started to protest that this was out of the question.

'But, Mrs Rees,' he said, 'she will never even recognise you as her mother. She is so severely retarded, she will never be able to give you what a mother wants from a child. It would be a mistake to hope for it.'

'But I'm getting it now,' she said. 'No matter what little she can give me, I love her. I love what's there, as I love my other little girl . . . there's no difference. You say she is giving me nothing, I say she is giving me something and I'll settle for what little she has to give.'

'Why don't you think it over,' Professor Bobath persisted gently. 'Leave her here, at the hospital. That is what I would advise you to do.'

He sincerely believed he was advising her in her best interests, she could see that. In his view, Paula was a hopeless case; Jan had her life to live. But she replied, 'No way. I can't. I won't.'

Very well then, he said. The department functioned three times a week, Monday, Wednesday and

11

Friday, and she could attend at her choice.

Jan left Harperbury feeling desperately alone. She reported back to Eddie, and his reaction was exactly as hers had been. He would never give Paula into care.

So the treatment began, every Monday, Wednesday and Friday for almost five years. Jan always had to take two children to the hospital with her. First it was Paula and Kerri. Then Kerri started school, and by that time Jan had Ian, so then it was Jan, Paula and Ian.

Because Eddie's shifts at the London docks, mornings one week, afternoons the next, meant he couldn't always be there with the car, it was arranged that transport for hospital visits would be provided by kindly Red Cross volunteers – a mixed blessing, as it turned out.

At the hospital Jan observed other patients, many in their twenties, some dreadfully misshapen. Perhaps, she would tell herself, this was because they had not had physiotherapy early enough in their lives; possibly the treatment hadn't been available twenty years earlier, perhaps their parents had kept them hidden away and this was the result . . . disfigured, limbs twisted, unable to walk.

Jan's thoughts went round and round. It needn't happen to Paula – surely she didn't have to grow to be as damaged as these people. There was treatment now, and so much more known in medicine. Surely she'd at least be able to walk just a little.

Jan prayed, too, without understanding why or to

whom. She had no sincere religious convictions, although they had had Kerri baptised. In her prayer, and it was always the same prayer, she asked that one morning she would wake to find Paula had become a normal, healthy child.

She was learning at the hospital that there are degrees of cerebral palsy. Paula's was the most severe. Her eyes rolled, and she had no co-ordination, couldn't swallow, and suffered spasms of stiffness so painful that she had to be prescribed Valium. She cried all the time, and this crying was the most distressing thing of all to witness because it indicated unbearable pain – not just the pain of the spasms, but also the pain of just living. It was many years later that Jan came to believe that Paula was also crying at the utter frustration of her life, at having no way of communicating. She was screaming in anger.

Now, when Jan thinks of those early years, it always brings tears to her eyes. 'If you are in a house with a child who cries all the time, what does it do to you? I don't know how I coped, I was just twenty years old at the time.'

It would have helped to have someone to talk to, but who? Not her GP, when she knew he had thought her neurotic. Not her mother, to whom she deliberately played down her problems. And not Eddie, who persistently maintained that Paula would 'catch up'. Far from reassuring Jan, Eddie's words only served to drive a wedge between them.

'That was probably our worst period, looking after a toddler and a baby who was a full-time job. Paula never slept through the night, yet we just ploughed on. I've always kept my problems to myself, however unhappy I felt. Eddie can't handle the emotional side. I always had the attitude that I'm making too much of things and mustn't. If I had ever broken down and cried, then I would be ashamed for making a fuss – just get on with it. I lock things away.

'Life revolved around Paula because it had to. Perhaps with hindsight you could argue that the other children should have been protected from Paula's problems, shut out from that. But if we had (not that it occurred to us that we should), then I don't think the family would be as close as it is today. I see Kerri every day, Ian phones every day to say, "I love you." Adam [her fourth and youngest child] has never asked what is wrong with Paula, she is just Paula.'

And so Jan loved Paula, accepted her, fed her, played music to her and kept her as comfortable as she could. 'In the house I moved her from room to room. If I went into the kitchen I'd take her too, often I'd sing along with the radio and do a little dance and I'd say: "Don't you think Mummy deserves a little smile for that? Smile, you miserable little cow, smile! Come on, give me something back." And later she'd give me this little noise, a sort of mewing.

'I remember the first time Paula smiled. Suddenly her face changed. I saw this smile break through, it was marvellous to see. I sat in the chair, crying with emotion and I could imagine how ridiculous this would seem if I said to someone, "Today she

14

smiled and I cried for an hour." People wouldn't understand. After all, a smile comes so natural with babies.'

In 1972, Jan became pregnant with Ian. She hadn't wanted another child so close, but it had happened and it was a case of getting on with it. As her pregnancy advanced, there was an urgent problem she needed to resolve.

CHAPTER 2

Sometimes (a poem for Mum)

Sometimes I'm happy
Sometimes I'm sad
Sometimes I'm lonely
Sometimes I'm glad

But as long as I have you
I will always love you

For as long as I have your love
I can see good and I can see fun
Free from trouble, free from harm

For take the sun and take the moon
You will always have my love
Which will go, on and on, Mum

A day without you is lost
And pointless to live
So I will gladly say goodbye

One of Jan's classmates at school had been a girl whose eyes crossed. She'd been the butt of other children's cruel fun, and an object of pity with the kinder children. Jan had pitied her. Now she was reminded of this girl, and was determined to discover what could be done about Paula's eyes, which rolled to the point where she had become boss-eyed. After persisting, through her GP, she finally arrived at an appointment with the eye surgeon. He explained that Paula's eyes rolled because of her condition: she had no control over the muscles that held the eyes in place. Jan asked whether an operation would correct the squint.

'Certainly,' he replied. 'But there would be no point. It won't make her see any better, and she'll never read.'

'She's almost two now,' Jan insisted. 'She won't know she's having an operation: this is the right time to do it. I'm expecting a baby – better an operation now than when we have the new baby to look after.'

'True,' the surgeon said, 'but I cannot see any point in doing the operation. It's purely cosmetic. And as she is severely mentally retarded, she isn't

19

going to know that she's cross-eyed.'

'But *I* bloody know she's cross-eyed,' said Jan. 'And it might make her see better. Look, when I deliberately cross my eyes it makes me see two of everything. Her eyes are swivelling around all the time, crossing and uncrossing, it must make it very difficult for her to see clearly.'

'Mrs Rees, I don't think you understand . . .'

'I'm no doctor,' said Jan, 'but I'm looking at her, and she's cross-eyed and I don't like it. And I'm sure when she's grown up she won't like it either.'

So eventually, because Jan refused to take no for an answer, he agreed.

And it was while Paula was in hospital that Jan and Eddie realised there was more to Paula, that the medical definition of her condition as being so mentally retarded that she was mindless, little more than a vegetable, didn't quite add up.

According to the surgeon it was a comparatively simple operation. After removing the eyelashes, the eyeballs would be lifted out, the muscles at the corner of the eye socket would be tightened, and the eyeballs would be put back. Paula was to stay in hospital for two weeks following the operation, for meticulous postoperative nursing.

Jan and Eddie organised a rota. Eddie left the house at 4 am, drove to the hospital to give Paula her breakfast, then left for the docks to start work at 7 am. Jan, after delivering Kerri to school, went straight on by bus and train to the hospital and stayed for the rest of the day. Her sister Kim collected Kerri from school and dropped her off with Jan's mother. At the end of his shift, Eddie would join Jan at the hospital, and stay until Kerri's bedtime.

Jan was soon aware that when she left the ward for any reason, Paula cried, and only stopped when she came back. Similarly, when Jan and Eddie were due to go home, Paula would start screaming, and Eddie would cradle her in his arms and walk up and down the ward, as he did at home when she wouldn't settle, singing his favourite John Denver song, 'Rocky Mountain High', until she fell asleep.

The rest of the time, Paula's crying was as it always had been; but this crying for something outside herself was new. As usual, Jan kept her thoughts to herself. Then came the morning Eddie was delayed, and arrived a little later than usual. Even before he'd reached the ward he could hear Paula yelling her heart out. A flustered nurse, trying to placate a very hungry child, was clearly relieved to see Eddie. 'Thank goodness you're here, she's been creating a big scene, won't let anybody else feed her . . .'

And Eddie reflected how curious it was that, if 'she's just a cabbage', she would know who was feeding her.

Three days after the operation, Jan and Eddie were told they could take Paula and nurse her at home. Her eyelids were stitched together, and she needed to have drops trickled in at the corners, which Jan administered. After a week, the stitches were removed, and it was found that the operation had been a complete success.

21

The fact that she had recognised them was a discovery for Jan and Eddie. 'But of course, knowing us didn't alter the fact that she was mentally retarded. After all, even the most retarded people know their Mum and Dad,' says Jan. 'So she knew me, she knew Ed, she knew she was out of her environment. And I knew that recognition was there. It made me question the original diagnosis. What if they'd got it wrong?'

A month later, on 14 December, Ian was born. Paula was then two, and still had not learned to swallow properly. Jan devised her own feeding method. Everything went into the feeding bottle; then, with a towel wrapped around Paula to hold her arms to her body and prevent them from flailing about, Jan used her free hand to angle the bottle, position the teat that had had the top cut out over the baby's open mouth, and literally pour. Paula would usually cry throughout. Sometimes she was sick, sometimes she seemed to be choking and Jan would have to stop, to pat her back. 'It was horrible for us both, but I just persisted. It took a long time for just one feed.

'Then one morning I got up, prepared her breakfast as usual, sat her on my lap and wrapped the towel around, and for the first time she didn't cry. It was as if at last she had learned to swallow. Up until then, that spasmodic reaction, recoiling at food or someone's touch, was something she did all the time . . . as she still does, if the wind hits her face or she hears a very loud noise.

'A few days later . . . my Mum had opened a tin of

Heinz spaghetti to eat with toast. "Try her with some of this," she suggested. "No way, Mum," I said, but I tried and Paula seemed to like it. And so we made progress. After that, when I prepared meals for the family, I included Paula. I sprinkled some sugar even on meat and veg because Paula wouldn't eat anything savoury – horrendous really. Very gradually, bit by bit, I reduced the sugar and she grew used to different tastes and flavours. She never learned to suck or use a straw.'

Such minor incidents were major milestones in the Rees household.

The thrice-weekly hospital visits had taken on a new element of adventure. Jan, plus two or three children, one screaming nonstop, plus a double pushchair and all the paraphernalia that goes with small children, did not add up to the ideal load for the ageing drivers who formed the backbone of the Red Cross volunteer service. One stalwart (who often asked Jan, sitting in the back, to identify the colour the traffic lights were showing) drove with blissful disregard of other road users.

Throughout these death-defying journeys Jan smoked feverishly to calm her fears. On one occasion a wild swerve caused her to drop her cigarette. Panicking at the prospect of a burning carpet, she snatched at Ian's bottle to dowse the smoking butt with milk. Ian screamed. The startled driver turned. Seeing smoke, he pulled into the kerb, dashed into a shop and came back brandishing a large jug of water which he hurled into the back of the car, filling Jan's lap and soaking the children.

It was when Jan reported back that the driver that day had gone the wrong way round a roundabout, and Eddie had to confront the reality that this was his entire family they were talking about in that car, that he went to his boss and arranged to be put on shifts which left him free to drive them to hospital.

And so he was there the day a nurse who had befriended Jan offered to show them the residential wards. She led the way, proudly pointing out the new layout, the fresh paint, the improved privacy. Patients now each had a curtain to make a cubicle for their beds – even a locker beside each bed for personal belongings. The sight of the silent occupants filled Jan and Eddie with deep sadness. The nurse, who had said that she believed their decision not to place Paula in the institution was correct, nevertheless was proud of the facilities the hospital had to offer, and kept pointing out the improvements, unaware of their increasing dismay.

Eventually, they reached a locked door at the end of a long corridor. This room was always locked, she explained. The children in it had severe behavioural difficulties and had to be kept away from the other wards.

The room had a high ceiling, high windows; the walls and floor were covered with a padded lining. Children lay, sat, shuffled, stared out through the bars of cots, rocked to and fro. There was a pervading smell of urine.

They pictured Paula in all of this, the stuff of nightmares. They left that day, a sad little group.

Kerri was with them and even at her tender age had understood. 'We would never leave Paula there, would we, Mum?' she asked.

At home, life continued to tick over. Jan looked after the house and the children, cooked economical stews and pies, suet puddings and cakes. Eddie came home from work, then went out; one night football, one night football practice, one night training. He needed his relaxation. At home, he helped out as best he could. He accepted Paula and the constant crying. All babies cried: he was prepared to put up with it. Throughout, he stuck to his conviction that Paula would somehow get better, but when and to what degree? Perhaps by the time she is ten she'll be improving, he'd say, by way of encouragement; but he said it less often as the months passed. Jan and he avoided conversations that begged too many questions and opened too many sores.

Jan had no illusions. At the beginning, she hoped that someone out there would be able to help her. Someone who would talk, and listen, and know the answers.

Her parents were there for her, given the demands of their working lives. They even gave up their home so that Paula could have a better start in life. It had been suggested that a garden would be beneficial for Paula: certainly anything would be better for a young family than having to trail small children, shopping bags and pushchairs up to the sixth floor. But the council's rule was that with two small children, their existing accommodation was sufficient, and there was therefore no reason to move.

Eddie's workmates on the docks had started to buy their own property in a new estate in Kent, Snodland, where prices were affordable for their bracket, and Jan and Eddie began seriously to consider moving out to the Kent countryside and a house with a garden.

They mentioned this to Hilda and Roy. Hilda said, 'What would you think about swapping?' This solved the problem with ease and re-established Jan in her childhood home. And it kept the whole family close. Until her death from cancer after a two-year illness, in 1978, Hilda remained Jan's closest – if not her only – friend.

This was vital. Having a disabled child sets you apart. Even that most fertile seedbed for friendship, the school gates at home time, yielded nothing. 'I used to take Kerri to school, and collect her at the end of the day, and none of the mothers would acknowledge me. I think they pitied me because of the way my life was, and I didn't have time for small talk. And because of the way my life was, I wouldn't have had any small talk to contribute.

'There is this sense of isolation. You're different from everybody else and people isolate you. Now I don't need those people, it does that to you.

'When people in the street saw my turquoise twin buggy I had bought in the charity shop, they would think it was twins and stop to have a look, and then they would see Paula and turn away.' Even invitations to take the children to family events at the working men's club stopped, as Eddie and Jan decided that basically Paula was an embarrassment to Eddie's parents, that people don't want to sit next to you when you've got a child like Paula.

Jan's desperate need to talk to somebody about her life with Paula led her to contact a woman doctor with two children, one with cerebral palsy, the other a Down's syndrome child. Jan accepted there was little likelihood of the two women establishing a lasting personal rapport, but the doctor usefully introduced her to the Gateway Club, a voluntary organisation for the disabled with regular social evenings. It was somewhere to go on Monday nights and Eddie was always happy to oblige, helping out with the transportation. Before long he was on the committee and became the regular driver, doing the rounds every Monday evening, collecting young people to deliver them to a school hall for an evening of dancing, table tennis and games, and driving them home later.

It was around this time that Jan's weight began a steady and remorseless climb. Her strenuous lifestyle, with three small children, housework, pushing the buggy, always walking (Eddie took the car to work and in any case, Jan didn't drive at that time), was no match for the calorific volume of her cooking. She found comfort in the kitchen, a cosy, solitary place, where she was in control and everything she cooked came out right. Eddie ate everything she put in front of him – but it was Jan who gained weight.

One day, a nurse at the Harperbury physiotherapy unit was making kind, reassuring remarks of the 'always look on the bright side' variety.

She got on to Eddie. 'Just think how lucky you are to have Eddie,' she said. 'He's a wonderful man. And with Paula and your weight problem and all, you're so lucky that he's stayed with you.'

It was to be the first of many such remarks.

'You've got that to cope with,' pointing at Paula, '*and* you're overweight. You're lucky your husband hasn't walked out . . .'

'Three kids and one of them like that,' a knowing nod in Paula's direction, 'it's surprising your husband's stayed with you . . .'

Even meetings organised for the express purpose of helping people in their situation seemed to inspire admiration for the way Eddie stayed with Jan – 'Most men would have walked out, you know . . .'

Jan recalls this time. 'So I had this mental block in my head: if I complained too much, as well as what I was coping with, Eddie would do what they all said, walk out. And soon that became, "Why does he stay with me anyway? I've got this child and I'm fat . . . I'd better not rock the boat." '

Eddie, a quiet presence during our conversation, said: 'I feel I was selfish. I think I should have encouraged Jan to talk more about it. I just helped out as best as I could.'

CHAPTER 3

For Jo

Need me Jo
I love Jo's love
I cry Jo's tears
Feel often, for my friend
Keep believing forever
Don't you lose your belief

Feel my life with envy
Count your love with songs
See, do not ever let her leave
To you I believe even love helps
Find your answers
Don't want your last book
From us a most future book

Jo Collins was a born performer. At two, her stage was a garden table in Enfield where she would regale the people in neighbouring gardens with renditions of advertising jingles, of which her favourite was 'The Esso Sign Means Happy Motoring'. As the applause died down, the diminutive Jo would ask: 'Would you like another one?' And they'd all reply, 'Oh yes, please' – or that is how she remembers it.

Nora and Harry Collins gave Jo's natural exuberance free rein. Forty years on, her primary school teacher (a staunch Chicken Shed supporter) still recalls Jo standing up in class and introducing herself with her Esso song.

During family celebrations, if the restaurant happened to have a band (Nora and Harry liked a restaurant with music), Jo would always offer to sing, and her brother would always kick her leg under the table. He alone found her performances cringe-making, and he made this obvious, despite being ticked off by their parents for being a spoilsport. Jo eventually learned when to stop, however irresistible the band.

Jo's grandfather had sung at the Royal Opera

House, which was the only obvious link with Jo's talent. Yet neither parent ever regarded Jo as exceptional; they just thought all kids could sing and harmonise, given the chance. There was always a record playing on the record player in the evenings and at weekends – they enjoyed all types of music, including Perry Como, Frankie Vaughan and other pop artists of the day.

Hand in hand with Jo's musical ability was a strong entrepreneurial streak. At five, she used her John Bull Printing Set to produce tickets, which she then sold to the neighbours for a show called *Cavemen's Troubles*: story and songs by herself, interval refreshments by her mother. Jo performed all the singing parts while her friends, enlisted very much against their wishes, had the acting parts – they weren't, in her opinion, very musical. Sweeping in and out of the French doors through the long curtains, turning the lights on and off, it was all wonderfully exciting.

Putting on shows became a regular event at Jo's house. They were performed either indoors or in the garden, with stalls set up for selling odds and ends collected from the drawers. These were her driving instincts and still are – the desire to sing and the love of organising.

In those days, most houses had a piano, and Jo's mother liked to sit at theirs and ponder what might have been had the war not interrupted her musical education. It was decided that Jo and her brother should have piano lessons, which both of the children hated, not only because the piano teacher was

so strict and practising scales was so boring, but
also because it meant – in Jo's case – having to miss
out.

You came home from school, had your tea, and
immediately had to go into the room with the piano,
alone, and practise endless scales while all the
other children were outside playing. You could hear
them, but you weren't allowed to join them. Being a
very sociable child, Jo wanted to be out there too. It
didn't seem right to her that she wasn't enjoying
this music. Up until the age of five, singing and
being applauded for it had been great fun. Now,
learning to play the piano was a very serious occu-
pation. She had to go to a lesson every week, usually
got told off for not practising her scales, couldn't go
out to play. Her brother gave up when he was eight.

By the time she went to senior school at eleven, she
had given up piano lessons and was playing drums in
her own band, which also included a pianist, guitarist
and bassist. Her hobby was not encouraged at the
convent grammar school, where guitar and drums
were dirty words and pop music considered to be even
dirtier, and where her entrepreneurial skills were
permissible only when a concert meant raising
money for school funds.

Her first song, performed in front of the entire
school at morning assembly, was called 'Death'.

Why do we have to die if we're happy on this
earth?
Why do we have to die condemned we were
from birth?

33

Lyrics were never her strong point – however, the nuns loved it.

Coincidentally, she found that by putting poems and Shakespeare to music, she was able to overcome her difficulty with memorising – asked to recite by heart, she had to sing the words. And the timing was fortuitous. Folk clubs were beginning to appear on the scene, so Jo formed a duo with a close schoolfriend, Mary Ann Clarke, both playing the guitar and singing. They became well known locally. Many pubs had back rooms which did service as folk clubs, where the custom was to set aside half an hour during the programme for 'floor singers' – people who came forward to perform. Jo and Mary Ann never missed these opportunities.

The atmosphere in a folk club was serious: chatting was not encouraged. And the material was equally weighty. Folk people traditionally wrote about a grievance – slavery and environmental destruction were favourite topics. Jo and Mary Ann tended to write about love, and were somewhat frowned upon for this; but it did not prevent them from being invited back and booked to play.

They found it all wonderfully exciting, appearing regularly in twenty local clubs without having to venture into London's West End. They were fifteen before they travelled that far. It may not have been entirely safe for two such youthful performers to go so far afield, but times were different. In the world of folk the people tended to be gentle, and in any case everybody knew each other.

Jo and her partner were earning a little, even

collecting a following. It was an excellent start, and their double act lasted for four years before they decided to change direction. Teaming up with two young men, they called themselves Distant Folk and performed songs styled on Bob Dylan's, with drums and bass guitar and more harmonies. It was a more commercial approach.

They made a brief but ambitious foray into clubland, which began when they were booked to appear on Fridays and Saturdays at a club called Cage d'Or. By night this was a discotheque, with a separate café where musicians performed. Next door was an empty building, formerly an elegant gambling club called (with great originality) Casablanca. This empty building struck the group as such a waste that they would berate the Greek manager who owned it, whose response was always a resigned shrug. Until, that is, the group came up with a scheme which would definitely make money. The manager agreed, and they were in business.

The venture became a gambling club with music. The manager provided the gambling, and his waiters carried up the food from his existing restaurant next door. Jo and Mary Ann did the bookings, calling the venue Live at the Casablanca, and ran it as a weekend spot.

Former customers were lured back by the gambling, but the entertainment was for everyone and the music drew its own audience. Live at the Casablanca ran successfully and profitably for four months until the demands – including being arrested and detained by Hampstead police for illegal bill posting – proved too much for the two, especially as this was the first year of Jo's catering course.

When Jo left school at sixteen with several O levels, knowing that she desperately wanted a career in music, she was also aware of the precarious nature of the business. Luckily, her skills weren't solely musical. As a little girl she had daydreamed of one day owning a restaurant and doing all the cooking. She had always been encouraged to cook, and had even made the front page of the local paper when she won a young person's cake-making competition at the age of only five. So cooking was the obvious second string to Jo's bow, and she duly enrolled at Hendon Catering College.

She finished the course experienced in the agony of waitress's feet, the drudgery of shift work in large hotels and the venom older staff can vent on trainees. She also knew how to make and decorate a cake to grace the smartest wedding, a skill she believed would stand her in good stead – as we shall see, she was proved right.

Meanwhile, her music had been ticking over, college permitting. So when her reply to an advertisement in *The Stage* for a country and western singer to do a summer tour of the American bases in Germany brought first an audition, and then a job offer, it seemed the perfect opportunity (this, despite the fact that she wasn't sure what country and western was).

Those two months spent in Germany working

around the American bases were to prove pro-
foundly distressing, however. She witnessed racial
violence between American blacks and whites; was
extremely ill; experienced the harsh side of the
music business, with the coarseness of life on the
road and exploitative management, an unpleasant
mixture balanced only by the inherent decency of
the hard-working musicians and the sheer delight
of making music. She regards the fact that she kept
a diary for the only time in her life, before or since,
as proof of her unhappiness at that time.

When she was asked to stay on at the end of her
two months, she answered with an emphatic no
thank you, and vowed that whatever she was going
to do in the future, it would be on home territory.
(Yet such is Jo's natural optimism that she accepted
the first foreign booking – to entertain holiday-
makers in Tenerife – that was offered.) And within
'the worst two months' of her life she describes a
satisfying scene: walking into a bar on an American
base, and hearing for the first time on the juke box
the recording by the Carpenters of 'Close to You', a
year before it was released in the UK. Jo got a
handful of dimes and just played it over and over
again. She decided she wanted to sing like Karen
Carpenter, whose voice was of a similar register;
she admired the quality of the harmonies and melodies, the beautiful arrangements.

The Germany interlude over, Jo and Mary Ann –
today a successful artist – continued their musical
career together, forming a group called the Music
Room, working abroad, and making a folk album

that got into the charts. They were contracted to Decca. Dick Rowe, the man who turned down the Beatles, was then head of Decca, and he took them on at the suggestion of guitarist Brian Daley, who produced them, wrote songs, and went on to make his fortune writing *Postman Pat*.

The icing on the cake came when Jo and Mary Ann were taken up by Radio 2, working three-hour sessions recording songs that the BBC used as and when it needed. One happy moment was recording their version of 'Goodbye to Love', a Carpenters song. Everybody was convinced it was Karen Carpenter singing, and Jo felt highly flattered.

Doing Radio 2, word spread. Jo was making a good living, although the money was secondary – like so many musicians she considered herself lucky to be earning money for something she would have done for free. Her career was climbing; her success looked watertight.

The Collins family were regular worshippers at Vita et Pax, their local Roman Catholic church, which was a former Benedictine monastery. Jo was asked to take over the organisation of music for the folk mass, as it was generally becoming known, a device aimed at attracting young people to attend church.

Jo's views on music in church were very simple. If people came to church to be prayerful, the music should not be a distraction, but something to assist prayer. Having to listen to a bad musician created exactly the opposite mood. There was no point in a policy of giving everyone an opportunity to play, if this meant including someone who couldn't play his or her instrument properly.

She had already noted the excellent flautist, Anthony Filby, and gradually she began to draw up a list of performers from the talented musicians she had been working with. They became involved because they liked her; she unashamedly chatted them up into taking part, and they found they enjoyed it. As a result, the standard of music at the church was brilliant. But as is often the way with folk and rock musicians, they were completely unreliable as far as attendance was concerned; occasionally Jo would have to go out with the pianist to guarantee he would be there. Jo herself was a constant presence, sometimes with a big band, other times with just her guitar.

The folk mass at Vita et Pax was a fortnightly event, more pop than folk; and as its reputation grew, people came to mass from miles around. It was even featured on TV.

It was the time of the religious rock operas *Jesus Christ Superstar* and *Godspell* and Jo and Anthony, jumping on that bandwagon, wrote a musical, *Rock*, about the life of St Peter. The music was vibrant, the direction (according to Jo, who was the director) absolutely hopeless, with the cast making up their own dances. However, it was so well received by the audience at Vita et Pax that it got a second airing, this time in the Notre Dame Hall in Leicester Square. Cardinal Heenan, Archbishop of Westminster, was in the audience, and he praised it to his goddaughter, Mary Ward.

39

Mary, twenty-nine, was a schoolteacher married for three years to Manus Ward. They had a baby son, Paddy. In her choice of career she had followed her own mother, Doris O'Dwyer, a teacher who rose to become a headmistress. The product of an East End working-class family, Doris – known as Dot – became the first in that family to go to grammar school, become educated and 'go into education' as Mary still describes it. Dot was by all accounts an inspirational woman: teaching was her natural vocation, and her influence was and is a driving force in Mary's life.

Patrick and Dot married before the war, and had Mary, their only child, comparatively late in life, when Dot was forty. It was a loving household. They continued to live in the East End, in a rented house, and when Dot was made headmistress of Barley Lane Infants School, Ilford, she saved up and bought a house in Sussex which they used for holidays. Mary still owns this house and does much of the writing and creative planning for Chicken Shed there. As if by some benign providence, her mother's gift continues to be a part of Mary's life and work, making its own contribution to the growth and direction of Chicken Shed.

Mary was sent to convent school, which she hated, so much so that all her subsequent working life as a teacher was spent putting into practice a philosophy that was the direct opposite of the convent's. A clever, self-motivated pupil, she was not an obvious target for the bitchiness to which the nuns were prone, but her inherent rebelliousness, her need to see fair play, put her at odds with their system. At the same time, she understood why her mother chose to send her there. Dot herself had been educated very happily by Ursulines (not the same convent as Mary's). Also, as a full-time working mother, Dot needed the security they offered, the extra back-up of a place where Mary could safely wait if Dot was delayed at the end of the day. By this time Patrick's health was cause for concern; after being demobbed from the army, he suffered a breakdown from which he never fully recovered.

His family had come over to England when he was a boy, as had the Heenans who lived nearby. Both families had known each other in Ireland and had strong ties of friendship: one of the Heenan sons, John, who had entered the priesthood, was Patrick's best friend, as well as having been a good friend of Dot's since before she met and married Patrick. And so when Mary was born it was inevitable that Father John Heenan should be her godfather.

Even as a little girl, Mary recognised the special quality of her parents. They and their friends were different, interesting; debate was part of daily life, and politics an ongoing subject. Her maternal grandfather, active in the Labour Party until he died, had been one of its pioneers back in the days of Keir Hardie. The church was at the heart of their lives, and even though Mary resented this as a child, she had no way of avoiding it. The embrace of the church seemed to her a stranglehold. Mary recalls once going to confession when she was ten years old and, after saying her 'Father forgive me for I have sinned' and listing her sins, the voice on the receiving end said, 'Yes, Mary, and would you kindly give a message to your father for me . . .'

Later she very much eschewed contact with the church, keeping it at arm's length even when she was teaching at a Catholic school. While never actually losing her faith, she acknowledges its fluctuations. At the time she was growing up, the church had not yet come around to encouraging questions from its flock, or certainly not in the circles in which her family moved. Among 'cradle Catholics' it was very much a case of doing as you were told: go to mass and you're sure to go to heaven. Somebody like Mary, who had a questioning mind, strong opinions and the attitude that she had a perfect right to speak, was not at ease with a teaching that set so many limits. Yet as an adult, she discovered in her godfather a valuable person to talk things over with; his answers to questions made sense.

Mary was early on committed to righting the wrongs of the underprivileged, and because of this she nursed ambitions to become a lawyer and fight against injustice; many years later, in fact, her son Paddy carried the same Free Nelson Mandela torch. But at seventeen, and in the sixth form, Mary changed direction. Father (by now Archbishop) John's niece Jean had four children, of whom the third, Michael, was a Down's syndrome child. To help Jean cope, and at the same time assist many other local families, Archbishop Heenan formed a group for children with handicaps (not a word you will find in Mary's vocabulary today, but common in the sixties), which needed young, energetic volunteers.

Mary and the school became involved, taking groups of children to football matches, concerts and social events. She had in any case known Michael since he was born. Now she was to meet other children with special needs, and as her involvement, interest, affection and friendship grew, so she saw that irrespective of their different abilities, they were more or less the same as the other children she knew. Because she found it all so enjoyable, she decided that this was where her future lay.

In the event, Mary never did work with children with special needs. She went to teacher training college, became a teacher and fell in love with teaching. Her first class consisted of forty-eight ten-year-olds, with that age group's expected range of ability. Some couldn't read. As Mary taught, she learned about herself, established her own attitudes and values. She hated the power structure of teaching, and refused to read out in order the children's examination results (grading was compulsory as Redbridge, her borough, retained the eleven-plus) or award stars for marks. Any recognition of achievement had to be wide-based. This was something she had learned from her mother, not her convent school, where academic excellence through discipline was the method. Mary believed in self-discipline, not, as she had experienced, discipline imposed through fear or even cruelty.

Mary's school, St Augustine's, was in any case nothing like the convent she had attended. Parents referred to the teachers there as 'the hippie staff'. They were all in their twenties, newly qualified, wore jeans to school, permitted pupils to call them by their first names on leaving day, and at times were a little wild, even for the broadminded headmaster.

At St Augustine's Mary found how much she valued teaching. It gave her a huge sense of achievement, and she revelled in her genuine love of children and people generally, and in working with them. Mary is still in touch with some of those early pupils. By contrast her own schooling, dominated by the convent ethos of being constantly put down and made to feel no good, had led her to have quite a low opinion of herself.

She had always loved the theatre, ever since being enchanted by *West Side Story* at fourteen in the West End. She had also thoroughly enjoyed being part of the drama department at teacher training college. So teaching was not just vital in itself; it also provided a forum for testing her ideas about drama, not only with her class but with the entire school, including the art classes. Given that this was 1969, the projects were highly ambitious and drew attention. Her school evening drama club was so successful that the local authority's drama adviser asked Mary to run something similar for children throughout the borough, which she did in the nearby former Doctor Barnardo's home (in its final stages of winding down).

While she was teaching it had struck her that through drama, children experienced break-throughs in understanding that they may never have achieved in any other way. Mary also felt that believing in individuals on the whole meant that they would come up with the goods – that you might be disappointed in people sometimes, but that on the whole you were never disappointed with every aspect of them or their behaviour.

This period at St Augustine's was a glorious, happy time for her, and when she stopped teaching to have her son, Paddy, she missed it terribly.

Mary, Manus and Paddy Ward moved house. By coincidence, the vendor of their new home was a Catholic schoolteacher. Seeing Mary's full names on the contract, Mary Angela, she said, 'That sounds like a Catholic name.'

'It is,' said Mary.

The vendor said, 'Then let me give your name to my church and I'll let them know you are moving in.'

In spite of having a cardinal for godfather, having her wedding in Westminster Cathedral and having Paddy baptised there, Mary had not involved herself in parochial life. So when after less than a week in the house, somebody from the church rang to wish her welcome to the parish and ask whether she would like to get involved, Mary was not forthcoming.

Nevertheless, a list was duly dropped through the door. The one item on it that seemed attractive (or, as Jo was later jokingly to describe it, 'least nauseating') was the Junior Youth Club, which met on Monday nights. With a husband who played rugby or trained in the evenings, and a small baby – not the undemanding sort to bundle up and leave quietly sleeping in the corner of the club house – Mary spent several evenings alone each week. And because she was missing teaching she thought, why not give this youth club a bit of a whirl?

Thus, on 4 February 1974 Mary went to Vita et Pax, and then into the church hall where the youth club were meeting. It was Jo's evening to teach guitar. Mary knew about Jo, that she supervised the music for the group mass which she had attended, and had found to be brilliant; and already had tremendous admiration for the young musician.

They were introduced. As they started talking, everything they had in common poured out – their interest in the theatre; the rock musical Jo had written and produced; Jo's singing and writing of music, and the fact that she was already using the youth club as a vehicle for her writing; Mary's love of working with children through drama. It all added up to an immediate bond.

They talked about having a theatre company where everyone could join in. You wouldn't have to do an audition, pay, or think you were anything special. You'd just have to want to do it. The two were centrally concerned with getting the right values across to children. They would do original work, make the piece fit the people, not the people fit the piece.

As their idea grew they decided they wanted a big

barn in the country where they could set up their own theatre. Jo knew a local landowner, Lady Elizabeth Byng. So she went off to tell her about their plans, and returned with the barn in the country – except that it wasn't a barn, it was a chicken shed at Dancers Hill Lane in Barnet.

Within a month of meeting they had started Chicken Shed. They had begun by saying they would call themselves the Lady Elizabeth Byng Theatre Workshop, but Chicken Shed just rolled easily off the tongue.

The partnership of Jo Collins and Mary Ward was to have far-reaching effects on the lives of thousands they had yet to meet. Their rapport was instant: by the end of that first evening in the church hall, Jo knew that she had met her soulmate.

Jo Collins: 'Generally, my memory is not good, but everything about that Monday evening is vivid. We were all standing around in the kitchen having a cup of tea and she walked through. She was wearing a long black duffel coat. I wondered who she was, I hadn't seen her before. A guy who was standing at the door introduced her: "This is Mary Ward, she's just moved into Clifton Gardens."

'We got talking. It was easy to talk. And she said that she directed things at her local theatre workshop and at school, so for me she was exactly what I was looking for. You could say heavensent. And then the next week she came, and we talked specifically about the music I'd been working on with flautist Tony Filby, and agreed that she must meet him, and

we'd play her some music. By this time I realised we
were soulmates.'

Jo was twenty-one (Mary twenty-nine). 'To meet
someone at that age and know this is someone I can
one hundred per cent trust was such a strong feeling I just wanted everything to happen there and
then, all that we aspired to do. I never had any
doubt, and I was right.'

They met once a week, later to include weekends,
with Mary's baby son Paddy in tow. Her house
became the office. Manus, initially perceived by Jo
to be 'a shadowy figure in the background', turned
out to be totally, unselfishly supportive, generously
providing a home for the planning side of Chicken
Shed and absorbing its growing demands with quiet
pride.

Working with Jo and Mary were Tony Filby and
Jo's friends Sally and Peter Heath, who had
co-written *Rock* and had eight children, who immediately became members of Chicken Shed. The
youth club numbered thirty teenagers, some of
whom allied themselves to the new group and at
once they set out to establish a junior Chicken Shed
group, as experience had taught Mary that working
with teenagers meant overcoming many preconcep-
tions, and the way forward was to start from an
earlier age. One of the many characteristics she had
in common with Jo was that they were both radical
– Mary in her approach to theatre generally, and Jo
in music.

In the techniques that were evolving in Chicken
Shed, Mary recalls, 'the mix was so radical but

the people weren't completely up for it.' For example? 'A dance: you don't necessarily have to start on your feet, but they expected to do exactly that. Six steps to the left then jump in the air, that sort of thing. I'd say, "Let's get down on the floor, start from a lying-down position", and they would be uncomfortable with that. But when you start with kids you don't have to cross that barrier.'

There were no overheads because the shed was free and the office was Mary's house. They had first-class costumes from day one because Mary's friend Joy Hollick (who quickly became Jo's friend too), a court dressmaker who lived nearby, became involved, and her two children Graham and Angie joined Chicken Shed. Profits from the productions covered the cost of materials.

The books just about balanced. If it is true to say they were always faced with financial problems, there likewise seemed always to have been people who came along when the going was tough, got involved, helped, and changed things for the better. As Mary says, looking back over twenty-two years, it has always been a big struggle, but there again they have always had the right people there, at the right time.

The combination of Jo's entrepreneurial skills and musical talent, and Mary's vision and confidence in dealing with large groups of people, was the drive that enabled them to set up so quickly, and that kickstarted their subsequent development.

Within weeks of their first meeting they were in business with *Isaac*, performed over Easter. Jo's wonderful 'musos' were much in evidence – many were already well known, some would go on to become famous in their field, such as Kevin Savigar, Rod Stewart's keyboard player, and guitarist Laurence Juber of Wings. This was followed, in August, by *Chrysalis*, a musical about growing up. Chicken Shed were delighted, if somewhat surprised, to hear later that *Chrysalis* had been noted, and that their company was singled out for the Most Promising New Company award from *The Stage*.

The company had used the shed for three years when Lady Elizabeth handed over the estate to her son. He promptly made a clean sweep of everybody not earning money for the estate – which, in fairness, was beginning to shrink around them – and the company were forced out, to become itinerant. The original church hall was now too small, so they moved from one church hall to another – two in Barnet, one in Whetstone, two in Finchley. They were usually lucky with the deals they struck: one was paid in kind, with free concerts in lieu.

From the beginning there was resistance to some Chicken Shed principles. Why must the work always demand original material? Wouldn't more people come to, say, *West Side Story* than to a play with an unknown title? And not everyone was prepared to take on the demands of Chicken Shed, where there was always a production in progress.

Chicken Shed took over Jo and Mary's lives, fuelled by a driving passion which always propelled them forward. Mary: 'We always knew it was life's thing. It is hard to know if someone had sat us down and said, "Now where do you see this going?" if we could have predicted the outcome, but neither of us are the sort of people who approach things as secondaries. I suppose it cut other things out of our life. It did kind of take over.'

CHAPTER 4

Do not let the anger

Do not let the anger and the sadness of the
   people make you different

Say that you will always stay the same
Forever knowing, forever believing

We are losers in the game
And if we don't know how we feel
No one will know how laughing can seal
So let them speak of sadness and joy
For hope will win again as long as there is hope

Paula was five, and there had been no mention of school. Every other child starts school at five; Kerri's notification for a school place had arrived in the post several months before her fifth birthday. Where was Paula's letter?

Jan rang through to the education office at the town hall, to ask what they were doing about Paula. Well, shuffling of paper, not a great deal, actually. But leave it with us, we'll get back to you. Then, silence.

Try again. She told them: 'I'm not a mother who wants to get rid of her child. I'd have her here at home with me all the time, but I'm the mother of a child who needs to get away from her mother!'

They said, 'You see, Mrs Rees, Paula being so handicapped, and also so mentally retarded . . .' 'Yes, but she's got to go to school,' said Jan. 'All children do, that's where they learn things.' They assured her that someone would look into it, come up with a suggestion. Then, silence again.

It was during the Easter holidays that Jan made one more call. Not so much a call as an ultimatum: 'Either you find Paula a place in school, or first day back I'll get her dressed, take her to school with

Kerri and leave her there.'

Immediately a place was found and Paula was enrolled at Hornsey Centre, a school for mentally retarded children, some also with physical disablement and in wheelchairs, like Paula. Jan, having checked out Hornsey Centre, knew its reputation. The headmistress was a brilliant American woman (who, unfortunately, soon afterwards returned to America), the building was bright and modern, and the school was buzzing with enthusiasm. This was where Jan wanted Paula to go; she would not have settled for less.

One of the first things Jan said to me when we met to discuss this book was: 'I was a different person then, when all this began. The woman you're seeing, talking to, you probably think I'm assertive and outspoken . . . quite aggressive really. When I met Eddie I was a quiet, trusting person, not exactly shy but I didn't ask questions, I believed what I was told, that the doctor was God, that people with education knew better than I did, that there were rules about what you did and didn't do which you never questioned, rules like you didn't have sex before marriage . . . sounds silly now, doesn't it, but that was the background I'd come from.

'Now when it comes to Paula I'll argue with the Queen if I have to. I realised I had to fight for her, because nobody else was going to do it, and because of the pain of it Eddie cut himself off from that side of it completely. He was always there to drive me to the hospital, to feed her, change her but not the fighting for her, he couldn't handle that, he didn't want to get involved in the emotional side. So I had to do the fighting. I don't trust anybody, in any profession, priest, doctor, teacher, I've learned that.' Over the months I developed an affectionate regard for Jan's battling instincts, her defensive response to any potential threat. Experience taught her to accept nothing at face value.

Having managed to instal Paula in the appropriate environment, Jan was frequently disappointed at the lack of any noticeable progress. In fairness, Paula was difficult. She did not conform to the image of helpless, affectionate, submissive disablement. She screamed, she bit the hand that fed her and other children in her range, she spat out her food – 'Because she wants attention', Jan would say when all of this was pointed out to her. She was not an easy child, the school staff said; she was truculent, prone to ferocious temper tantrums, strong-willed. At home she was both adored and understood, responding to Jan and Eddie, Kerri and Ian, Hilda and Roy with her radiant smile. She would roll on the floor, reaching out, sometimes making contact with things she wanted to play with. Jan saw the staff exchange that look when she pointed this out, a little knowing smile, disbelief. 'Mrs Rees, she knows nothing. She doesn't know you, she smiles at you because you have a happy voice, she likes that. But she doesn't know who you are.'

Over the years, spending so much time within the institution, Jan and Eddie learned that the greatest problem, from Paula's point of view, stemmed from an aspect shared by most caring organisations:

nomadic staff. Carers moved on, and it was the children who had to adapt to new people, new methods, new ways. The new carers, too, had to learn, from scratch, the individual signals of the young they cared for. The child was left with no one person on whom he or she could rely for continuity.

Knowing Paula had no means of communicating, Jan and Eddie were constantly on edge if she was out of their sight. There was, for example, the one and only holiday away with the school, a week at the seaside. It even had a title: A Bucket and Spade Holiday for the Mentally Handicapped. Jan and Eddie agonised for weeks over whether or not they should let her go. They knew well enough the reasons against: their own anxiety at having her out of their protection; the possibility that she might be taken ill, or wouldn't eat, or had an accident (dislocated bones and joints were a natural hazard); the chance that she might feel unhappy or frightened. On the other hand, why should she miss out on something other children took for granted – a school outing – especially as she would be the only one? Besides, it promised to be stimulating and (the thing that finally tipped the balance) Paula's own favourite carer would be there.

So Paula went off in the school bus, and Jan and Eddie spent a miserable week, Eddie in particular becoming distraught with anxiety. Had they known the favourite carer was not in attendance, and that due to some muddle they had been misinformed, they would no doubt have driven off and brought Paula home. They knew, without a word spoken, that they would never put themselves through that again. And they didn't, until the time several years later when, cushioned in the bosom of the church, Paula visited Lourdes.

During that Easter in 1975, when Paula was waiting to start school, Chicken Shed presented their first production in a proper theatre. If the Rees family noticed the posters advertising the production at the Intimate Theatre in Palmers Green, it would not have occurred to them to buy tickets. After all, theatre wasn't for the likes of them, as they'd be the first to tell you. In the event, *Alice* was a sell-out, and the people who filled the seats were not the mums, dads, grannies and aunties of the cast, but the bona fide theatre-going public. The production made a profit for the company. Mary's second son, Joseph, was born the same year (the third of three momentous February births – Paddy 1973, Chicken Shed 1974, Joe 1975), and thereafter Mary would say she had three children, Paddy, Joe and Chicken Shed.

CHAPTER 5

Dad

Dad, life is good when you are in it
Life is sad when you are not
Life is better for you
Life would be bad if not
Life is good with you

Money, or the lack of it, was the greatest strain on Jan and Eddie. When Eddie went to work at the London docks, a closed shop operated and only men related to existing dockers could get in, so it promised high rewards and jobs there were at a premium. Eddie and Jan looked forward to the good wages; but barely had Eddie settled in than the great heyday was already on the ebb: work petered out, and the docks struggled and died, victims of intransigent union practices and shortsighted policies. The warning signs had been ignored.

From the time Paula was seven, up until she was ten, when they were really badly off, Jan worked evenings at the local hospital, on the wards, earning £21 a week. When they needed £800 to buy a chair for Paula, they had to resort, in desperation, to sending out an SOS in the local newspaper. As horrendous as going out with a begging bowl seemed to them, they knew they had no choice.

'We've never had any spare cash,' Jan told me. 'Because of having a severely disabled child and putting our lives into her, we've achieved a beautiful daughter. In fact, more than that, Paula is a gift to us. So we have four beautiful children, but financially we've scraped through. And she's worth every sacrifice.'

Their tastes and requirements have always been modest. On the basis of what you haven't had, you don't miss, Jan maintains that like her and Eddie's parents, they've never 'had money' so they don't know the difference. They still use the same things in the house that they had when they were first married; they couldn't 'just go out and buy a new washing machine'. They are always looking for ways to save money: secondhand shops and car-boot sales are the Rees's hunting ground. Eddie made Paula's bed to save the cost of buying a new one.

When Jan fantasises about winning the lottery, it is in terms of buying a house each for Kerri and Ian and doing up her own, the former council house where she grew up. The front room, recently redecorated, boasts a handsome reproduction Victorian fireplace purchased wholesale through the kind offices of a friend's son, who is in the building trade. As Jan says with a laugh, it is 'the biggest Victorian fireplace the street had ever seen'. She is very proud of it.

But why not a new house, rather than renovating the old one? 'I'd never move. But,' the fantasy gathers momentum, 'I'd trade in my caravan for a bigger one, a three-bedroom model. My caravan is my escape. I'd find it very difficult to be without that now. Another bedroom would be lovely for Paula, give her some privacy.'

We exchange ideas of luxury. Jan's would be to stay in a hotel with all the family, and have meals provided. Just the once. 'You know, a hotel holiday like some families have. We never did that.' A few years back, in pursuit of this 'real holiday', she applied for the Weymouth tourist guide, sorted out everything with a wheelchair sign and ended up with two big hotels and two B&Bs. They did their sums: even the least expensive represented about six months' spare money. Project abandoned.

Every year they had a holiday. They would load up the car with all the camping gear, then get out the map and ask the children to pick the direction they wanted to drive. Up, down, left or right.

Since they didn't begin packing until Eddie got home from work with the car, they would be heading off around midnight. There was no telling how far they would drive or where they would end up. They reminisce fondly about relentless rain in Wales; or the car breaking down on a steep hill somewhere in Dorset and slipping away with Paula's pram strapped to the roof rack; of tents being washed away; of being threatened by a hostile herd of cows into whose field they had inadvertently ventured, tent pegs at the ready. Adam missed all that, as he was born in 1983, by which time they were progressing from camping to caravans.

A friend lent them a touring caravan for a fortnight to see how they got on with it. They were enraptured: after tents, this was comfort. Another friend offered them the use of a caravan on a farm. They turned up to find it knee-high in weeds and nettles, covered with green rain mould. Excitedly they scrubbed away at the mould and the shiny aluminium emerged. They were hooked on caravanning, and before long managed to find a secondhand caravan at a price they could afford and installed it on a caravan park at Clacton, on the Essex coast, which has been the site for every holiday and all possible weekends since.

Snapshots show them always smiling. They are such an engaging family you would expect them to make friends wherever they went; but they say no, people on the campsites were not friendly. 'Because of Paula, people were embarrassed, didn't know what to say, so kept away. It didn't bother us.'

There was, however, *one* holiday episode which bothered them – Jan in particular. They were visiting underground caves in Kent and had asked permission to take Paula in, as the entrance had a 'No pushchairs' sign. The man at the pay desk said they would have to leave the wheelchair outside, so Eddie complied and carried Paula in his arms. The children found it hugely exciting, down in a lift, out into a long dark corridor, deep in the bowels of the earth, with twisting tunnels, darkness, more lifts – this time going up. By the time the guide had stopped in a cave to give his talk, Paula was so excited she was starting to make her little squealing sounds. The crowd seemed to find this amusing; in any case, there was little anyone could do to stop her, as the sounds were involuntary squeaks of pleasure.

Eventually the guide stopped his lecture, and addressing his remarks to Jan and Eddie, said: 'I've had enough, this is very distracting. Please leave and go back.'

They tried to protest, but he was adamant, so they had no choice. But as if the humiliation wasn't bad enough, the route back was far more difficult, with three children and Paula still being carried, no one to lead them, and a pervading darkness. By the time they reached ground level, Jan was ready for a fight and tackled the man on the desk. Although she eventually extracted an apology and a refund, you get the impression that nothing short of locking up the guide in his cave overnight would have mollified her.

Bingo afforded Jan the occasional night off. After she went out, Eddie would get out his LP of Strauss waltzes from the 'Music You Know and Love' series, put it on the record player, and they would all dance around the room, Paula in her father's arms. Sometimes he hugged all three, telling them to close their eyes and imagine the castle ballroom, the chandeliers sparkling, all the people in their fine clothes. Kerri has only to look at that same record today to be instantly transported back into her childhood, the happiest times, to relive the mystery and excitement of those evenings. Invariably Jan would return to find all four fast asleep on the sofa.

One evening she came home to find Eddie anxiously waiting. Paula had been crying. He had managed to settle her in bed, and eventually she had fallen asleep, but he was still worried about her. Jan went into the bedroom; Paula slept in a cot beside them, as they couldn't leave her alone at night. Even now they wait until she is asleep before they themselves go up to bed, and Eddie will sit up until three in the morning if necessary.

When Jan lifted her, she could see her femur unmistakably sticking out at an odd angle. So straight to hospital, Paula wrapped in a blanket. As the staff in Casualty checked her, it became apparent that certain leading questions were being asked, that not only were the nurses and emergency doctor treating Paula's injury with suspicion, but that they, her parents, were presumed to be possible culprits in this. Jan and Eddie had assumed the injury must have happened during the day at school, perhaps while she was being lifted. Paula was so prone to injury, and it didn't immediately dawn on them that they were being seen as the perpetrators who had actually injured her themselves.

Fortunately, Jan and Eddie had only just grasped what was being implied when a senior doctor who knew the family appeared on the scene. They saw from his expression that he was setting the record straight.

Paula's leg had to be put in traction, which meant a lengthy stay in hospital. That wouldn't do for them – they wanted her home. Somebody in the children's orthopaedic department recalled a patient the year before, a boy with a leg injury, whose father had built a bed with a wooden wedge which created the same effect, uplifting the leg and keeping it straight, as would the hoist used in hospital. They tracked him down. He still had the bed, and kindly donated it for their use, so Paula was allowed home.

But the matter didn't end there. The initial alert

had been noted by social services, and a social worker was duly appointed to check their story of an accident with Paula's school. At the same time, the social worker checked out a few theories of his own – on what sort of parents they were, for example: after all, they were under considerable pressure. Were they safe with Paula? Was the reason they wanted her home for Christmas because they had broken her leg and felt guilty?

By all accounts, school authorities had swiftly sent the social worker packing. Jan found out about this visit at the time, but not about the nature of it. That, she only heard about years afterwards, when a retired teacher who had stayed in touch with her told her that the staff had agreed among themselves that Jan should be kept in the dark 'because we thought you would have killed him. It wasn't worth the upset, then.'

He stayed around, however, and not as a reassuring presence; after Paula left hospital and came home to the special bed, he would sit for hours, silently watching the family going about whatever families do. Once he asked: 'Why did you have her home? Why didn't you leave her in hospital and have a nice easy Christmas?'

'Because we wanted her here, because she's our family,' Jan replied. What a daft question. He said he thought that was strange. Jan thought *he* was strange.

It was obvious he was trying to analyse them. 'What are your plans, long term?' he asked. There was no answer for that. From the time they accepted Paula, as she was, they knew they could never plan. People often asked what they would be doing next year, as if next year would bring some solution, and they would be presented with a choice. Their only way was, and is, to take one day at a time.

When Paula was nine, she needed an operation to free her legs, which were 'scissored' – that is, they crossed each other at the hips and were frequently dislocated. When this happened, Jan and Eddie would immediately go to the hospital, wait hours in Casualty for a doctor, and by the time they were called, the hips would have gone back into place. The condition caused excruciating pain, and because Paula was unable to sit properly she would balance on one haunch.

Mr Moynaugh, the orthopaedic consultant at the hospital, always described by Jan as 'a darling of a man', was gentleness itself. 'If I give you this injection you aren't going to love me any more,' he used to say to Paula, as he charmed away her fears. They lost count of the number of visits and admissions; hospital was an ongoing feature of life.

He decided to unscissor the legs and straighten them. The operation involved cutting the tendons in the groin. The legs were then set at right angles to the body, sticking out one each side, and set in plaster against a broomstick, also in plaster to guarantee rigidity and hold the legs firmly in place, wide open, like an upended crucifix. Jan stayed with Paula in hospital, and after ten days they went home together, Paula to recuperate. Eventually the broomstick and plaster would be removed and the legs allowed to draw back into a normal position. Because of the ungainly way her legs had to be, they bought a huge pram in a secondhand shop and wheeled her around in that, stretched out across the top.

CHAPTER 6

We need each other

Every person has to be dead
Who does not believe in someone

I believe in you
I want everyone to be happy
Like I'm happy with you

I want everyone to be beautiful
Like you're beautiful to me

I play around
and you still stay with me
I stay out late
And you keep wanting me
I keep doing bad things
And you go on loving me

We need each other
We need each other, like songs need words

Paula's feet were in plaster too, and because she was in so much pain and consequently wriggling, when they took the plaster cast off, her feet were a sorry sight. They had been rubbed raw, the backs of her heels so appallingly that Jan felt physically sickened.

With the plaster removed, Paula's legs remained stuck out on either side, and needed gentle massage to relax the tension and encourage the blood to circulate. Jan began to do this loosening-up physiotherapy at home, and would sit with Paula on her lap, facing away from her and out into the room. Now that her legs were no longer scissored, Paula was able to sit in an almost upright position, and as Jan massaged she would push Paula forward and back, at the same time rocking her from side to side, all the time singing or chatting, to distract her attention from the pain.

One day – one particular, shocking, heart-stopping day – Jan was flicking through the pages of a magazine thinking about Paula, her child, the child she knew. This was a child who knew her mother, knew her dad, understood what it meant to be happy, knew what it meant to be sad; she was adored to bits, and she was absolutely, categorically, severely mentally retarded with not the faintest hope of improvement. Every expert had said so.

As she massaged Paula's legs, Jan began to read to her just as she would read to a normal child. 'Look, Paula, lovely chocolate cake, Mummy's favourite.' As Jan spoke, Paula leaned forward towards the magazine and touched the picture of the chocolate cake with her nose.

Jan lifted her back, assuming this had been just an involuntary movement. She turned the page, another picture. 'Can you see the cat, Paula?' Paula leaned forward and pressed her nose to the cat's photograph.

Another page. 'The flowers, Paula, pretty flowers, where are they?' Again Paula leaned forward to the Interflora advertisement and touched the flowers.

Jan's heart started to pound, thoughts screaming through her head. Perhaps it was just the big pictures; what about the small pictures? She turned the pages, choosing small objects in big pictures, small pictures on pages of words, of hairspray, curtains, beds, an exercise bicycle, a fountain pen, a garden wheelbarrow, mind racing ahead as she tried to grasp what was happening, desperately wanting someone here, now, to see what she was seeing. Not to be alone, like this.

Some instinct prompted her to take the next step. Reaching for two pieces of paper, she wrote 'yes' on one, and 'no' on the other. 'Paula,' she said, holding up one piece. 'This says "yes". And this,' holding up the other piece of paper, 'says "no". Now you show me. Which one says "yes"?' Paula touched it. 'And

The family at home for the photographer from *Woman's Own*. Mark, Adam, Kerri and Connor are left of Paula; Ian and Nicky are bottom right; while Eddie balances Kyle on his knee, behind Jan.

Jan and Eddie in the summer of 1964 at the Coombe Haven Holiday Park, Hastings.

On their wedding day, 11 June 1966.

Paula, aged fourteen months, at Harperbury Hospital. Occupational therapist Frances Tubbs (left, holding Paula) suffered from a less severe form of cerebral palsy.

When a door-to-door professional photographer called one day, Jan couldn't resist the offer. Ian (three), Kerri (seven), Paula (five).

Paula on her sixth birthday. First the candles, then the bumps – she knows what to expect!

Eddie with Paula, on holiday in the Isle of Wight, 1978.

The mayoress of Muswell Hill spends a little time with Paula and her teacher Wendy during a visit to the school, 1980.

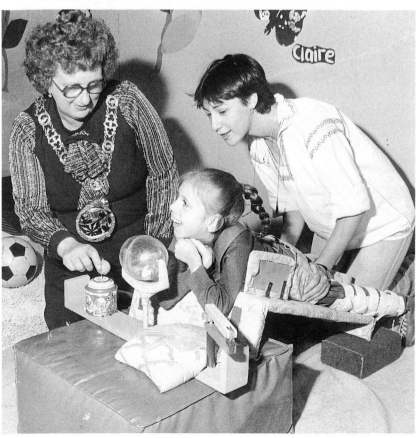

The school photo. This one is Jan's favourite.

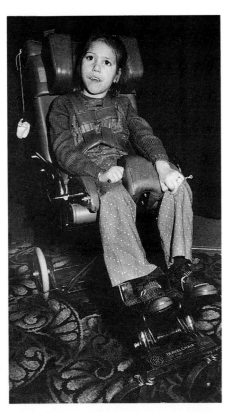

Paula, aged ten, in the special chair purchased with the funds family friends George and Brenda Harvey helped to raise. The last word in high-tech, the American-made chair doubled as a car seat.

The *Enfield Gazette* ran this picture of the Rees family to spotlight the wheelchair appeal.

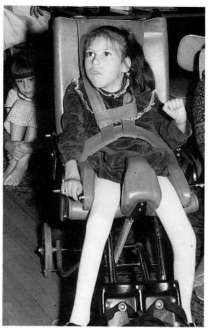

The annual holiday was always an important part of family life. At Pontins, near Cheddar Gorge, Somerset, 1980 . . .

. . . Walton-on-Naze, 1986. Jan and Paula by the sea on a blustery summer's day.

St Thomas's Church, Oakwood, 17 October 1987: Paula, pretty in pink, is bridesmaid to sister Kerri and Mark.

which says "no"?' She was right again. Jan mixed up the papers, playing games, testing her to see if she really knew the difference between yes and no. Paula was right again and again and again.

The implications were forming fast.

'Paula, if you lean to the right for yes, and to the left for no, you'll be able to communicate with Mummy, won't you?' And Paula leaned to the right for yes, and Jan pulled her back and hugged her and it was the most exhilarating moment of her life. They both laughed together, and Jan cried. Paula, leaning back into Jan's body, her head sideways on Jan's shoulder, wept silent tears.

Then Jan got out the snapshots and began the game again . . . where's Daddy, and Ian, and Mummy? Paula got it right every time.

Jan's mother had died just over two years previously. She found a family group photograph. 'Where's Nanny that died? Show me . . .' asked Jan. And Paula did. It meant that she remembered her.

Jan waited impatiently for the sound of Eddie coming home from work. As he stepped through the door, she wasted no time showing him what Paula could do. He watched in stunned disbelief. They needed to tell someone to share this. They dialled their best friends George and Brenda's number. 'Fetch her over,' said George, and the Rees family packed into their red Cortina and drove around.

George and Brenda watched, impressed. 'If she can read yes and no,' said George, 'then she must be able to read other words . . .' Cat, dog, you, me, dress, shoes, tree, drink, food, soap: they tried them all, starting with simple words for beginners and increasing to slightly more demanding words, such as soldier, policeman, friend, teacher, television.

Apart from the discovery that Paula could communicate yes and no, there was the mystery of how, without any initial way of communicating and without anyone ever attempting to teach her, she had learned to read. Jan and Eddie theorise that Paula's high IQ equipped her to pick up information and skills from what was on offer around her. In the same way that a child can recognise words from a familiar storybook while it is being read to them, she will have absorbed words from magazines, newspapers and television. She has never been able to pick up a book.

Jan and Eddie know also that Paula has exceptional hearing. Now, at Chicken Shed, friends remark on her ability, even in a noisy room, to eavesdrop on conversations out of normal range – she will sometimes be found laughing at something she has overheard at the far end of the room.

For the moment, this new development remained a glorious, happy thought for Jan and Eddie to ponder. Jan, particularly now, used her time with Paula to explore their developing understanding, an exciting game they could play for hours. Because Paula had no control over her body, her left arm always had to be strapped in to stop it flailing about, and her whole body was in a state of perpetual, trembling, quivering motion. It was not until she was ten years old, and the hip operation had almost corrected her posture from semirecumbent on one side to balanced sitting up, that she could lean in any direction; and that was only possible with Jan supporting her. By having her head held firmly in her mother's hands Paula was able to turn her head to the right and left, and shake it to give the 'no' added emphasis.

After a week of quietly and methodically getting used to this new situation, Jan went to the school to show them what Paula could do. She expected congratulations . . . astonishment . . . joy . . . something, at the very least professional interest. But there was virtually no reaction, other than a hint of patronisation. Ultrasensitive to the attitudes of what she always felt were her intellectual superiors, Jan could have misread the signs – except that the headmistress afterwards said: 'Even if we had believed you, what could we have done about it?'

'Just to have been believed would have meant a great deal to me at that time,' Jan told her.

This development (or alleged development in Paula's condition) went on record, and psychologists came to the school to carry out tests on Paula and Jan. They pronounced that in their opinion, Jan was subconsciously guiding her daughter.

'But what possible reason could I have for that?' Jan countered. 'I loved her the way she was before, mentally retarded with no brain like you've always said. Now if I know that she is intelligent, it's harder for me. It's harder to know that you have an intelligent child, locked away in there.'

The school set up an assessment panel. They sat around the large table in the headmistress's study, the psychologist from Harperbury Hospital with his team of psychology students, the physiotherapist, the headmistress, and Jan. They asked her questions, she answered through Jan. They said Jan was turning Paula's head, and possibly it appeared so, especially if, as Jan believed, they were in effect setting out to disprove rather than prove. And she was only too aware of that.

Six years later when Paula left the school, Jan requested and was given her records, and she read that on that occasion, Paula had been tied into her chair with elastic to test the degree of movement, and to disprove Jan's claims. This experiment worked in favour of their theory, not because Paula couldn't do what Jan claimed, but because she *wouldn't* co-operate with them. As a result of the wall of total disbelief confronting her, she had built up her own barrier. This annoyed Jan considerably; when Paula, having done exactly what was asked of her while sitting on her mother's lap would, five minutes later on another lap, play dumb.

Jan would implore, 'Come on Paula, why aren't you helping us, you know you can.' She could not understand why Paula seemed deliberately *not* to be proving herself. Today, knowing her daughter better, she can sum the reason up in one word: obstinacy. 'Paula will dig her heels in,' says Jan. 'And those tests annoyed her. Some were childish and she didn't like that, and took offence. They used toys . . . "Show me the brick, Paula, show me the fluffy teddy." . . . the sort of toys babies play with, soft toys. She was ten, she wasn't going to co-operate with that sort of thing, it was insulting to treat a ten-year-old like a baby. "Can't you see she thinks that's babyish?" I would say, but they'd look at me as if I was mad. Someone actually *said* I was nuts on one occasion . . .'

One part of the test, the 'note home', was tricky. It meant Jan would have to ask Paula questions relating to events at school that day, and record the answers. Even for parents with fully functioning school-age children this is unavoidably problematic. If Jan did not record the answers expected (sometimes because Paula had interpreted events in a different way) it was construed as proof that they were not communicating.

Paula meanwhile continued to demonstrate her own powers of control in her own way – through temper tantrums. She hated the obligatory dip in the school swimming pool, and used to kick up a terrific fuss, making it clear she wasn't going to be forced (which in any case was never the intention). Julie, her carer, a brilliantly intuitive woman by all accounts, said to her one day: 'How about going in first, before the others. Then you can come out when you've had enough.' Paula acquiesced, showing that the problem had been her reluctance to go in with a crowd of others; she had been afraid of that.

Independently, Jan contacted the Spastics Society, who conducted tests, and filmed Jan and Paula together. The Society expressed the view that in their opinion, Paula was definitely communicating. But then, unknown to Jan, they visited the school, and after observing Paula there, they reversed this opinion and told the school psychologist that in their view, Paula's 'breakthrough' was in her mother's head.

After that, Jan's will to fight shrivelled. 'I don't know if you can imagine it. You have this belief about your child and nobody else believes you. If the headmistress doesn't believe in you, the speech therapist doesn't believe in you, the psychologist doesn't believe in you, the doctors don't believe in you, where do you go?

'Before, I understood the limits. Now that I knew she was far more intelligent than we had ever imagined, I had to live with the knowledge that she was frustrated and bored at school and at home. What could I possibly do to stimulate this child? I had no skills or experience to handle this. I could try at home to the best of my ability, but she needed it in the school environment and she wasn't getting it.'

So she thought no more about it then – she had other pressing problems.

In 1980, the year that Paula was ten and learned to indicate yes and no, Andrew Haynes, a boy with cerebral palsy, was sent along by his parents to a Chicken Shed meeting at Vita et Pax church hall. Andrew liked it and he stayed. For the first time, Chicken Shed membership included a child with a physical disability.

Then, in 1981, Jo Collins opened a wine bar called The Greedy Grape to provide her with an income. The demands of Chicken Shed had now taken priority, leaving little time for pursuing work in the music industry. With Jo's skills and flair, the bar soon became the in place. The food was good, too: all those years at catering college had come to fruition.

And on 4 October 1983, Eddie's birthday, a brother for Kerri, Paula and Ian was born and called Adam.

CHAPTER 7

For Jo's birthday, 1995

Jo's my freedom
To keep saying to the world
Sit up, and listen

As the demands of Chicken Shed grew, Jo turned her back on her lucrative career in commercial music. The money was guaranteed, but she was becoming disenchanted with her once-beloved music business and wanted to concentrate on Chicken Shed.

When just beginning to put this book together, I once asked her if it had ever occurred to her that in Chicken Shed she had created something which dominated her life and demanded too much. She replied that on the contrary, she had never 'resented or regretted a moment. For me, my selfish thought was this is what I want from life, I never want it to go. I never had any doubts.'

Rather like taking holy orders? 'Many people who take holy orders don't know they've made the right decision. I have no doubt about my vocation. Chicken Shed is a microcosm of the world. It is a way through art and music and dancing of saying, "This is a philosophy of life."

'You can digest and understand through drama and music more than through listening to any number of politicians standing up making speeches. I don't think politicians very often move people to rethink their philosophy; personal experience does. We're educating not just in the skills of the theatre, but what we think is a pattern for life and through the children, the families too. Parents can't deposit their kids here like Brownies or horse-riding. They get involved, and once involved all the arguments fall into place.'

Both Mary and Jo needed to earn an income. Mary, when the boys were of school age, returned to teaching. And Jo had her catering training to fall back on, although she also knew catering to be the hardest work in the world.

The first two years of that course at the Hendon Catering College were spent in waitressing and kitchen work. In those days, London hotels limited the options for women working there to housekeeping and reception – other skills had to be learned elsewhere, so Jo was sent to Poole on the Dorset coast.

Kitchen life was a revelation. Many of the casual staff were one stage removed from down-and-outs, who had come to the seaside during the season for free accommodation. Fights were commonplace; knives were thrown about instead of loaded into the washer. Frustration was often directed at the faceless customer, seen to be privileged. 'To this day,' says Jo, 'I would rather eat in a small family restaurant than in a big hotel because I've seen what goes on in the kitchen, awful things put in the food as a means of somebody getting their own back!'

Trainees were disliked on principle. Most of the restaurant staff, from headwaiter down, had worked there for many years. Now, with no hope of getting a better job, here were these students training for management.

Every Saturday night the hotel had a dinner dance, which meant staff didn't finish until two in the morning. There was an option of Sunday work, either breakfast, lunch and dinner, or start at eleven in the morning and doing lunch, afternoon tea and dinner. Jo would never miss going to church in those days, and the nearest Catholic church was in Bournemouth, a serious bus ride away.

She conjures up a memory of going to the room she shared with fellow student Di, both girls sitting on the bed, crying with the pain of their overworked feet, as they soaked them in bowls of warm water and drank huge mugs of Horlicks, eight spoonfuls in each cup, so thick you could almost stand the spoon up. And all the while, tears of pain rolled down their cheeks.

She always had to get up too early. There was only one bus, arriving at church too early; then she had to wait for mass to begin. She always arrived back at the hotel late because of the bus timetable, and invariably received a public reprimand from the head-waiter, a scenario enacted every weekend.

One Sunday during afternoon teas, while carrying a huge loaded tray from the dining room, Jo fainted. Everything crashed, everyone stopped mid-sentence, mid-bite, and there was tiny Jo in a pile of broken china, scones, strawberry jam, clotted cream and fancy cakes, collapsed with exhaustion flat out on the floor.

It never occurred to Jo and Di to do anything other than soldier on. Both girls had been brought up with the ethic of not complaining, but sticking with it. Jo's father's business motto was 'If you don't make money it's because you're not working hard enough.' Di's father was also in business, and her upbringing was similar.

Unsurprisingly, when Jo and Di returned to college, they discovered that 95 per cent of their classmates had dropped out from their original placings because of conditions.

Jo chose cake decoration for her cooking experience. She spent this time working for the Queen's cakemaker, Floris, in Brewer Street, Soho. Every day she cranked up in an ancient, rickety lift to the top floor, where she laboured under the tutelage of a 'fantastic genius called Ron', who was deaf and a skilled lipreader. Enthralled, she watched him paint a copy of the *Mona Lisa* with icing on a cake. For an order to commemorate the moon landings, she assisted in creating a cake mimicking the surface of the moon.

'When I said goodbye to the course, I thought one day I'll come back to this.'

Looking around for a way to earn money, Jo thought she liked the idea of cooking again, and together with Mary's friend Joy she set up a home catering service. They were very quickly doing so well they decided they could expand from Joy's kitchen, and have their own premises. By the time they had found a suitable shop, rundown and crying out for expansion and redecoration, wine bars were in fashion. So they opened The Greedy Grape, a venture which incorporated the party catering business.

There was an initial hiccup, when Barnet magistrates' court rejected their licence application. It went to appeal at Barnet County Court, armed with character references, affidavits from women who said they would use a wine bar but not a public house, a statement from British Rail offering its space for car parking, a one-thousand-strong petition, and the legal services of the solicitor who had represented the opposition in the initial hearing. The judge, finding in their favour, congratulated them warmly and tendered his best wishes for their success and intention to visit at the earliest opportunity.

It was just as well: they were due to open the next day and had already taken delivery of all the glasses and the wine.

Success came. There was live music nightly in the basement, with Jo singing every Sunday. The wine bar had a very good run, and was by all accounts the talk of Barnet. But . . . there were problems. The first came when one of the three partners pulled out, saying it was too demanding. Later, Joy had to give up because of family commitments, and Jo took over with sole responsibility; she had to borrow money from the brewers to buy Joy's share. To cope with repaying the loan, as well as doing gigs, she extended opening hours. But in so doing, she unfortunately attracted a whole new class of trade, the roughs and the drunks. 'It was tough on the staff, and I spent the evenings after Chicken Shed being a bouncer in The Greedy Grape, chatting to people to make sure they didn't cause trouble.

'And I could look in the mirror and see the grey hairs and I thought, "I've got to get out of this." '

After eight years The Greedy Grape was sold.

The timing was oddly fortunate. Mary's illness was already in the wings, and Jo was soon to need all her time and energy to take over what Mary had been doing, and work full-time for Chicken Shed.

CHAPTER 8

Cat like accusing eyes

Saw looks
opening up other ruined eyes
Saw dreary lines
Tired upon me
Cat like accusing eyes

Look up, jotting, trying glances
Look glad, figuring out your disease
Leap up, jotting, other trifle wills
You misguide
or who wanders
Elevate your watching
or why please
It joins our outside view
Unity within grows I
True

Being awarded The Most Promising New Company accolade by *The Stage* had put Chicken Shed on the map, albeit as a very small speck somewhere, or a note on a list filed by producers and casting directors. Hence, in early 1982 there was a telephone call from London Weekend Television, then setting up a series entitled *Saturday Action*. The producer asked to see a couple of Chicken Shed teenagers; would Mary bring them in for an audition?

Mary replied that a couple might be a bit difficult. Could she bring in, say, four or five?

At that time they had around twenty-five teenagers, and she took them all. (Dave Benson Phillips, another hopeful who is now an established TV performer, was also auditioning. He recently confessed to Mary when they met on set during *Children in Need* with Terry Wogan, that he had been intimidated by that huge Chicken Shed presence.) The producer was sufficiently impressed to sign them up promptly for the entire series. Jo even wrote the theme tune of the series, and the group was filmed singing it. Chicken Shed earned a fee and it enhanced their profile. Over eight weeks, alternate Thursdays were spent recording the show in various parts of the South Bank and LWT studios. During those weeks every child got to do something in front of the cameras; and that included seven-year-old Andrew Haynes, the boy with cerebral palsy.

Travelling home on the Underground one evening after the most enjoyable, exhilarating, satisfyingly exhausting day, Mary listened to the group as their conversation turned to what being part of Chicken Shed meant to them. How they should be sharing this in some way, putting something back into the community. They talked about Andrew, how he had walked further that day than he had ever walked before, and what fun he had had. Then one of the group said: 'Where are the other kids like Andrew, the kids that can't walk? There must be more of them . . .'

That thought lodged in Mary's head. Where *were* the other kids like Andrew? They had 140 people in Chicken Shed at that time, but Andrew was the only one with any sort of disability.

Pestered by the kids who had first planted the idea (they wanted an answer and they wanted action) she began to make enquiries, and someone mentioned that the person to talk to was John Bull, who ran Cheviots, a local centre for children with disabilities and in the care of social services. Mary went to see him, and told him: 'We're a theatre company and we would like to involve kids with disabilities in the company.'

Already a pioneer integrationist, John Bull was looking for precisely what Mary offered: mainstream activities in which to place his children, whose ages ranged from babies to young adults. Chicken Shed fitted nicely.

'Great,' he said, 'here are some.' He indicated Cheviots was at her disposal!

They did not, at that stage, discuss the practicalities in any great depth. It was sufficient for Mary that her question had been answered.

Their first step was to take a group of young Chicken Shedders to Cheviots for a briefing on issues likely to come up, assuming that when these newcomers came through the door it would be a whole different ball game, and that they had better be prepared.

Mary and Jo set up a Wednesday session at Vita et Pax and stood by, on that first evening, having taken the precaution of having a generous number of regular Chicken Shedders to hand. Both Mary and Jo were undeniably apprehensive as they waited until it was time to open the doors. What had they taken on? What's more, would they be able to cope?

The kids from Cheviots came pouring in. 'We spent the first half hour feeling sorry for them – how unfortunate, how unfair, how sad,' Jo remembers. 'Then their enjoyment took over and it became apparent how talented some of them were, and that was that.'

By the end of the session, each Cheviots child was doing something he or she had never done before, and each Chicken Shedder was also doing something completely new. It was all novel, vital, valuable, and the course was set.

There were thirty newcomers on the first night. The numbers grew very quickly as word spread, and what soon emerged was that these young people with mixed disabilities were able to contribute to the work that they were doing, on every level.

'It was a shock,' says Mary, 'though not to John because he had already worked in this way and knew that people had all sorts of different abilities. But because we were so willing to listen to experts and assume that these kids did need special treatment – and in many ways a lot of them did because they had reached the age of sixteen or seventeen being treated in a certain way – it took a while for the penny totally to drop that we weren't actually doing anything different with them than what we did at any of the other sessions.

'In fact, it was after five years of doing this special group that we realised it was impossible to group people together in this way, disabled and able-bodied. The so-called disabled were as different from each other as the able-bodied were different from each other – it really was a group of individuals.

'And that's when we took the step of integrating across the board, and the Chicken Shed philosophy – that everybody is able to contribute and should be valued – was then being stretched to involve people that society does not usually involve in that way. Society itself doesn't believe that all its people can contribute to it; it believes that there's a section that will automatically achieve more, hence a lot of money goes into the education of the clever and able-bodied.'

At first, Chicken Shed was seen by many of the Cheviots kids as another place to hang around; it was particularly tempting for parents of children with disabilities because there was so little else available, and they seized on it as a social club. Today's younger mothers have no such misconceptions about Chicken Shed. They take their children there because they want them to be part of a mainstream theatre company, and because the evidence shows that drama ripens self-discipline, self-confidence and the ability to communicate.

As a remark from one of the Chicken Shedders had given Mary the idea to reach out and look for the disadvantaged, so that first evening Wednesday session planted the seed of integrated drama, and in turn, God and finances willing, will feed offshoots in other fertile places in the future.

CHAPTER 9

Christmas 1989

Have a heart at Christmas
So this world can see
How the good can send out
Songs of hope and love

Glad for the friendship
Glad for the sun
Glad for Dad
Glad for Mum

When Shubi Raymond came along to the Hornsey Centre, Paula was fourteen and a half. Shubi was the new headmistress; and hearing of her appointment, Jan lost no time in presenting herself at her office. She was at once charmed to be greeted by 'a beautiful Indian lady, charismatic – like Paula'. Encouraged by the warmth of the welcome, Jan explained what Paula could do. Shubi listened, displaying no hint of the usual disbelief. 'That's fine, Mrs Rees,' she said, 'I'll do that with her.'

The following day, after Jan had demonstrated how she worked, Shubi took Paula on her lap, spreading out the pictures and word cards. There was an instant understanding; Paula had very obviously taken to this new friend, the first person, other than her mother (she wouldn't work with Eddie) whom she had ever worked with. At this time, there was still no one outside the family who believed in Paula's ability, except Jan's friend Gwen Conroy, herself a mother of a child severely disabled and blind as a result of meningitis.

But there was no question of having to convince Shubi. Shubi was experiencing Paula's communicating skills first hand. Although the official view remained that unless Paula could communicate independently, rather than through a third person, the technique was useless, at least Jan was no longer the lone voice saying, 'If she can't do it independently, this way is better than no way at all.'

Jan happened to chance upon a magazine article about the Irish writer Christy Brown, who as a boy had taught himself to write after his mother had attached a pointer to his head. She rang Shubi, who immediately grasped the potential for Paula, and when Jan and Paula arrived at Shubi's office next day, two new members of staff were waiting.

Shubi introduced Winnie Dacre and Lois Terry to Jan and Paula. At this point, Paula's language still included only yes, no, and leaning towards letters and words with Jan or, to a lesser extent, Shubi.

There on the desk was the head pointer, its band far too large for Paula's tiny head. Shubi broke a piece off and Jan held it in place, its pointer protruding like a unicorn's horn. With Paula's chair positioned at the desk, in front of the electric typewriter, Shubi fed in a clean sheet of paper.

'There you go, Paula,' said Jan. 'Write your name.'

It took a while, but she did it. 'Paula.' Letter by letter. Unaided.

'Right,' said Jan. 'Now you can do it, and you can do it on your own. You can do it with Shubi and Winnie and Lois. I'm not writing with you any more.'

Then, taking a big gamble, she put on her coat and picked up her bag. 'I've had enough,' she said. 'I'm worn out, knackered, and I need a rest. Do some writing with them.' And she went home.

And Paula began to write. At the same time, as she wrote, she began to assert herself. The pen, or rather the head pointer, became the mighty sword. She caused trouble. 'Do you know, Lois,' she tapped out one day, 'that so and so thinks you're a shit?'

Poor Lois was understandably dumbfounded. Not only by the message, but the language! People tended, still do, to regard Paula as a child, all sweetness and innocence. Her face is angelic.

Privy to the most private conversations – the inevitable result of being treated as if she were deaf and dumb – Paula discovered the delight of repeating these indiscretions, to maximum effect. Initially, the recipients thought Paula's remarks were a one-off – until one evening when, sharing a drive home, Lois said to Winnie: 'If I tell you something off the record, will you promise not to repeat it? Paula told me . . . !'

Winnie listened, shocked, the more so because she had her own snippet to add: 'And Paula told me . . .' Thus they discovered that what each had taken to be a tactless comment inadvertently, even innocently, passed on was in fact Paula enjoying herself with wholesale scandalmongering.

But not simply that. Paula asked both Lois and Winnie to speak to Shubi about the backbiting, and the result was a staff meeting in the headmistress's room, a shake-up and some very embarrassed faces. It might have seemed drastic, but it achieved what Paula most wanted: to remind others that she was a living presence, not an inanimate object.

Or almost what she wanted. Paula wasn't at the showdown as she had hoped to be, and when she discovered it had happened without her she felt she had missed out on the best bit. So Shubi invited some of the staff back into her office for a good-natured encore.

Inevitably, there was lingering unease as people raked through their memories of things said in quiet moments . . . in the presence of this third figure in a wheelchair. How much of what she had overheard was stored in Paula's memory? It was clear that she relished the limelight that producing these mini-bombshells guaranteed, and had yet to learn tact and discretion.

Not only some of the staff were upset by Paula's coup. Her actions had also earned her the wrath of her sister Kerri, an occasional helper at the Centre who bore the brunt of being the girl whose sister told tales out of school. 'Mum, you've got to stop Paula causing so much mischief,' she said. 'I'm getting blamed because she's my sister. It's got to stop.' Although Jan couldn't help but see the funny side of it, she spoke sternly to Paula, and eventually the joke wore off and stop it did.

Since she was twelve, Paula had worn a brace to correct the curvature of her spine. The brace was the work of the orthopaedic department at Great Ormond Street Hospital. First they had made a plaster of Paris mould, and from that a plastic jacket which, for the next four years, she was to wear all the time, never taking it off except to wash.

The curvature in Paula's spine was S-shaped, and the prognosis was that it would, because of the damage inflicted on various organs of the body, eventually prove fatal.

But the brace had not arrested the deterioration in her spinal alignment. With the passing months, the curvature got worse. Her body was skewed to one side, and she needed pethidine daily to blot out the pain. She also had to be fed by nasal tube because spasms prevented her from eating normally, was frequently hospitalised, and suffered the effects of a spastic colon, which caused irritable bowel syndrome and vomiting. All in all, she was a very sick child: her life was wretched, and getting worse. If she was to live beyond the age of eighteen, her only chance was a spinal fusion operation to correct the curvature.

Mr Moynaugh arranged for an appointment to see a surgeon at Great Ormond Street Hospital. After a lengthy examination, he turned to Jan. 'I could operate but I don't want to, because she has a very small chance of surviving the operations,' he said. 'In fact, there is more chance of you having an expensive funeral than there is of your child coming out of this hospital alive. I must be very blunt with you, I don't want to operate on her.'

There was a moment's stunned silence. 'Do you realise,' Jan said finally, 'that she understands absolutely everything you say? You say she is mentally retarded – well, I say she isn't. She is intelligent, she hears you and she knows what you are saying.'

107

Whether or not he believed her at that time, the surgeon was evidently genuinely concerned not to upset her, irrespective of whether Paula's feelings were involved. He took Jan to one side, out of Paula's earshot, and described exactly what was entailed in correcting scoliosis. Because the operation took twelve hours, it had to be done in two stages.

'One – open up the front, collapsing the lungs and breaking the breast bone to reach the spine. We insert a metal rod with six screws to straighten the bottom part of the spine. Afterwards, the patient has to be kept lying totally flat on her back, drip fed, not moving, until the second operation two weeks later. This time we go in from the back, chip the hips to place a metal rod at right angles to the spine, to hold it straight and in place. If that doesn't straighten the spine, we might have to use bolts in her head.

'She will need two to three months in hospital to recover. Also, there is a serious risk of the lung collapsing. The main reason for not wanting to go ahead with this operation is that much of the recovery depends on the patient's mental state, the will and determination to survive; this requires commitment, mental strength. She doesn't have that mental strength.'

He put Paula's chance of surviving the operation at 10 per cent. Yet without the operation, she wouldn't live beyond the age of eighteen. Time was running out; it was a now-or-never situation, and if the operation was to be done at all, it had to be soon or she would be beyond surgery. The surgeon's professional judgement was that to perform such a distressing operation on a child (for that was how he regarded her) while believing there was minimal chance of survival would be callous. He repeated several times that he had no wish to inflict pain to no good purpose.

Both Jan and Eddie agreed that if there was only a 10 per cent chance of survival, they would take that 10 per cent. But the final decision must be Paula's. Back home, with so much to think about, Jan carefully spelled out the situation to Paula, explaining that because so much was at stake, so much pain to be endured, the choice was hers. 'This time it isn't up to me and Daddy . . .'

That conversation between them is sharply etched in Jan's memory. 'Paula knew everything, we didn't hold anything back, and she said yes, she wanted to go through with it. I promised I would be by her side, throughout, that I'd never leave her.'

The surgeon had not committed himself to doing the operation, and Jan and Eddie knew they needed help. Jan went to Shubi 'because Ed and I had worked out that people like Shubi and the surgeon speak the same language. People like Eddie and me don't have the right words to express our thoughts in a way that is acceptable in professional circles. I could beg and plead and get irate, but that wasn't going to carry the same weight as someone like Shubi speaking for Paula. The surgeon and Shubi are on the same side of the fence, they've had the same education.'

So Shubi went with them to plead their case. To

explain why she believed in Paula's intelligence and capacity for understanding, and to say that Paula had already demonstrated her strength of spirit, her love for life – she had been through so much, and she deserved this chance, however slight. Eventually the surgeon agreed, on condition that he first took Paula into hospital for three or four days' observation. Then he would make his decision.

Finally, they were told the operation had been given the go-ahead. It was to be a long wait.

Jan and Eddie had another pressing problem. Ian was in serious trouble at school. His difficulties had begun in primary school. Being dyslexic, he could never keep up with the brighter boys, and soon developed an image of himself as stupid. The more he failed, the more he sensed the teachers' antipathy, and the more he felt excluded. By senior school, he seemed always to fall foul of authority. He was struggling academically, disruptive, occasionally violent. At home he was gentle, goodnatured and especially loving towards Paula; at school, he was ready to fight anyone who made a disparaging remark about her drooling mouth or rag-doll body.

With monotonous regularity, Jan was summoned to the headmaster's office to thrash out Ian's latest offence. Only once did she query the accusation, when the headmaster phoned to complain about Ian's behaviour in the playground that day and request she come in to see him about it. Jan asked if he was sure the culprit was Ian. Usually it was pointless defending him, but this time it was different. Yes, said the head. He had seen Ian with his own eyes.

'That's odd,' said Jan, 'because Ian has been home with me all day, lying on the settee.' It was a case of give a dog a bad name with Ian: he was always to blame and he had got to expect it.

Jan's feelings about the situation bordered on panic. Ian seemed to be constantly up against the headmaster, as was another boy in his class, Paddy Ward. On one of their all-too-numerous school visits, Eddie and Jan once witnessed a boy jump out of a window and run off at great speed. Who's that? they wanted to know. Paddy Ward, came the reply. (Around this time, Mary heard 'Squee' mentioned once in connection with some classroom misdemeanour. This was Ian's nickname at school, and she wondered where anybody got a name like that.)

Jan sought help for Ian's behavioural problems and poor academic performance through the school, and was asked to attend a counselling session. Gratefully she agreed to go; she wanted to talk about Ian, and this was a start. But the counsellor wanted to talk about Paula and Jan, not Ian. 'Her theory was that Paula was at the root of our problems,' says Jan. 'And Ian was in such a state that I wanted to sort *him* out. She caused more of an upset, instead of calming things down.' The counsellor posed a question they had heard before. 'Tell me, how do you see your long-term plans?' There could be no answer. There was only today and tomorrow and the day after.

Almost a year had passed when word came in

111

December that the surgeon was ready to admit Paula. No, said Jan. 'If we're going to lose her, we'll have Christmas together, first.'

The stockings, the turkey, the Christmas tree (with the same lights and decorations as on their first family Christmas, rooted out of the same box). Paula was terribly ill, but Jan and Eddie soldiered on, working to make it seem a normal Christmas, not a special one. Jan's talent for putting things to the back of her mind got her through. Jan knew the worst – that Paula had only a pathetic hope of coming through the operation – but the other children didn't have to know. 'If I had gone overboard, made more of Christmas, made it that special Christmas to remember, always, they would have guessed. It was only a matter of days away . . .'

Ian had finally gone too far at school and had actually kicked down a classroom. True, it was a prefabricated mobile building, fenced off and ready for demolition; true, it already had a few holes in it; and true, he wasn't the only one. But he was the only one caught and identified, and as a result he was expelled.

On the day that Paula went to Great Ormond Street Hospital's Annexe, the Queen Elizabeth Hospital in Hackney, Kerri left home. She had taken, recently, to staying overnight with a friend. This time she didn't come back. There was no letter or phone call, just word through a friend saying not to worry about her, that she wanted to be on her own.

Jan and Eddie weren't angry, just sad. They

understood that this was her way of coping.

Looking back at that time Kerri, now a mother herself, says, 'I suppose I was the original wild child. I stayed away for four months. I felt I'd let them down, but I just had to have a different sort of life, away from the illness and the anxiety. All that worry and guilt . . . I loved my sister so much, and she was suffering and there was nothing I could do about it . . .'

At the Annexe, they took Paula in a few days before the first operation, which was performed on 26 January 1986. The second took place on Valentine's Day, 14 February of that year. They knew she was desperately afraid. In the car driving to hospital, Jan watched her in the rear view mirror. Paula was crying.

After they wheeled her down to the operating theatre, Jan and Eddie went out into the dark, wintery street and walked and cried. There were no words with which to comfort each other. The surgeon had touched her shoulder, lightly, kindly, a comforting good luck sort of sign, as they took Paula. He means well, Jan thought then, he is a kind man but he doesn't understand Paula as we do, he thinks she has no quality of life.

When they brought her back, she looked as if she were dead but the surgeon said she was all right, really, and the nurses stationed permanently at the foot of the bed were reassuring. Jan stayed, as she had promised, sleeping sometimes in a chair, sometimes in the hospital and, as the tension eased, in a nearby house which had been set up for mothers of desperately sick children. Several of those children died. Grief and bereavement were never far away, a constant reminder to Jan of her own precarious situation. Eddie, supported officially and unofficially by workmates, visited every day after delivering Adam, then two, to Jan's sister for minding. Ian was being tutored one to one by the kindly Miss Lewis, a former member of the staff at his school, and he took care of himself.

Letters, cards, gifts showered in for Paula, who was, it transpired, the smallest patient the surgeon had ever performed this operation on – because the patient does not grow after the spinal fusion, it is usually left until adulthood. Visitors and well-wishers called by; one, a former teacher of Paula's, now retired, travelled up from Devon. Her spirit and tenacity didn't fail. And Kerri came; a friend had kept her informed of developments.

Many times, Jan feared they had done the wrong thing. She talks about that, how her thoughts moved in circles as she sat with Paula, reading to her, talking, or watching her as she slept. 'She was so tiny, so frail, she weighed barely two stone. I cannot bear to think how we would have felt if Paula had died, knowing it was because of us that she was there. But now she's had ten beautiful years.'

They went home, Paula wearing a brace even longer than the one she had been wearing, and not to be removed. They put her bed downstairs in the sitting room. The hospital organised a daycare worker to call every morning and help Jan with the complicated nursing procedure. At the first sight of

Paula's operation scars, however, the carer took fright and stood rooted to the spot, terrified to touch Paula, and watching in horror as Jan completed the task before rushing from the room. Meanwhile, the Rees family were much amused.

Paula was confined to a reclining wheelchair, and gradually – very gradually, because she was still in considerable pain – they were able to raise the back of the chair into an angled position and eventually a sitting position. Kerri moved back home. Life settled down.

The time finally came around for Paula to leave Hornsey Centre and the teachers she had grown to love, and move on to the local Halliwick College for the Physically Handicapped – she was no longer classed as mentally retarded. Her great driving force was to write, however painful and tedious this process. For Paula, a good day was one page in five hours. Jan knew that when Paula wrote 'and a coffee' that she was signalling she'd had enough and it was time to stop.

One speech therapist was emphatically inclined to the view – which the Rees family had heard before – that since Paula couldn't communicate unaided, there was little point in working with her. The therapist said as much to Jan.

'She said that Paula sits in her chair thinking she is a poet and superior to everyone else . . . and I was very upset by her lack of understanding,' says Jan. 'She had a favourite child, one who could communicate easily. She liked a child in a wheelchair who smiled when you wanted it to smile, shut up when you wanted it to shut up, but Paula isn't like that. She also accused Paula of deliberately wetting in order to annoy her, but since Paula has absolutely no control then that couldn't be true. I still had the fear of people not believing in her. I worry now what she must have said to Paula when I wasn't there, if she said those things to me.'

That year, 1986, in The Greedy Grape, Chicken Shed was launched as a charitable trust. It now had a membership of 150.

CHAPTER 10

Happiness and a baby gave love

I am doing time
Open a mind not body
Being like this is going on forever

Before I was born
The life before me was different

Happiness and a baby gave love

Sunday, 13 March 1988 was the date Chicken Shed moved centre stage. On that evening in the church hall of All Saints, Whetstone, Judi Dench and Michael Williams played host to a gathering of guests invited specifically for their potential help and expertise in solving a problem. This was that Chicken Shed, growing bigger and bigger, meeting four times a week in various halls, storing costumes and props wherever a spare room or cupboard could be had, needed a proper home – badly.

Address books had been plundered and anybody known to be great, good, charitable, influential, well-connected, motivated, of generous spirit, rich or famous, and who might possibly help find a theatre, had been invited. It says much for the ties of friendship that so many gave up a cosy Sunday at home on an exceptionally cold, wet and windy March night to travel out to a north London church hall where water dripped through the leaking roof to splash into buckets below . . . in order to watch a suburban amateur theatre company they had never heard of, on the word of someone who probably wanted to extract money from them for this dubious pleasure.

Through Sandy Gonzalez, a Chicken Shed mother, Judi Dench, her husband Michael Williams, Pauline Collins and her husband John Alderton had become involved. Both couples had already been demonstrably supportive, Judi and Michael in helping to set up a trust to improve and manage Chicken Shed; and Pauline Collins, firmly believing that more people should see their work, in organising a show at the Piccadilly Theatre.

If Chicken Shed were to have a theatre of their own, then they needed money, and fundraising at this level called for a high profile. They needed help: this evening's appeal was the first step. The audience, the 'target' guests, were seated at tables with Chicken Shedders, who were not about to waste the opportunity.

After the performance, Mary made a speech outlining their needs and aspirations. To survive they must find a home: a permanent base which would give them room to grow and to spread the word further afield, to the greater benefit of the greatest possible number.

She told them: 'In Africa there is a saying:

If you can walk, you can dance;
If you can talk, you can sing.

At Chicken Shed we say,

Even if you can't walk, you can dance;
Even if you can't talk, you can sing.

Because singing and dancing are done with the spirit and not with the body alone.'

By the end of the evening, Lady Rayne had undertaken the task of raising the money to build a theatre.

On Monday morning, 14 March, Brian McAndrew, Chief Executive for the London Borough of Enfield, went in to work at the Civic Centre and dictated a memo to every chief officer saying: 'The London Borough of Enfield will find Chicken Shed a permanent home.'

And Lord Rayne went into his office and said: 'Find out about Chicken Shed. I'm very interested in helping them.' He had been chairman of the board of governors of the National Theatre for eighteen years, during which time he had overseen the transfer of that company from its original home, the Old Vic, into the new purpose-built theatre complex on the South Bank. He also had unrivalled experience in property development, building and finance.

He and Lady Rayne had attended the evening at All Saints out of the instinct not to let a friend down; Judi Dench had included such an appealing 'do try' note with her invitation.

Lady Rayne remembers it with total clarity. 'We avoid going out on Sunday evenings, and it was such a miserable, cold night, and I think we were also feeling unwell. But we went along and at once we forgot everything but the excitement and exhilaration of meeting those remarkable, selfless, inspired and inspiring people.

'We were touched, tearful. Driving home in the car we both said at once we wanted to help, and I started forming committees and spreading the word among my friends.'

Lady Rayne had been involved in charity work since her marriage, and knew how the wheels turned.

'It was slow at first, and then I decided to go for a big push, because we needed so much money, more than a million pounds certainly. At times it was quite daunting. I'd had no idea how big the building would have to be to house this huge talent, 700 members today with 1000 on the waiting list.

'Once you've made the connection everybody who comes into contact with Chicken Shed wants to help, wants to give, their time or their money . . . all ages. My four grown-up children are so supportive, as are their friends.'

Once Lord Rayne applied his own expertise the operation moved even more smoothly ahead. 'He gave his support by sorting out the financial matters and co-ordinating plans for building, and later the building work. Around that time he was leaving the board of the National Theatre, so it helped us a great deal.'

CHAPTER 11

As far as the eye can see

As far as the eye can see
As long as the land is free
With you by my side
Nothing can harm me

As long as you love and give
As long as you are free
As long as you live for the good
So life will be

College would soon come to an end; and then that was it, as far as Paula was concerned. What then? As much as Jan enjoyed having Paula at home, she desperately wanted Paula to meet people of her own age, make friends, develop some social connections like other girls of eighteen . . . or almost like. As it stood, Paula's only evenings out of the house, were occasional visits to the pub for a drink with Eddie and Jan – the last thing Eddie wanted to do, but it was enjoyable for her. They had had firsthand experience of social clubs for the disabled, where a person could be left sitting in one corner at the start and still be in the same place, having spoken to no one, when it was time to go. Paula needed something to stimulate and amuse her, and Jan began to ask around.

She heard about an organisation called Chicken Shed, which sounded interesting though vague, and came across a handbill in the library with a phone number. She called this often and unsuccessfully for weeks before contact was made, and when that happened she learned that they were holding an open evening and people were invited to come along to a session. It was April, a Wednesday. Jan's bingo night.

'You'll have to take her,' said Jan to Kerri. Jan's Wednesday bingo was sacred.

Kerri and her future husband Mark Brown, resplendent in punk – black leather for both; Kerri, her previously green hair now raven black, wearing chalk white make-up – deposited Paula at Vita et Pax, saying they would be back to take her home. They returned later, somewhat apprehensively; the place had struck them as a peculiar sort of set-up, if friendly, but they found Paula shining (Kerri's word – she always uses it to describe that occasion), clearly stimulated by her first taste of a regular Chicken Shed session. It was obvious to her sister that Chicken Shed had totally accepted Paula as an intelligent human being, and Paula by all accounts had displayed none of her usual shyness and reserve.

Mary was absent that evening, feeling unwell (in fact, she was seriously ill without knowing it) but had heard back from Jo about the new girl: 'You're going to love Paula, she's wonderful.'

Within days Jan called, and introduced herself: 'I'm Paula Rees's mother.'

'Paula was great,' Mary said. 'We're really glad she's joined Chicken Shed.'

'I thought you might be interested to know,' said Jan, 'that Paula writes things.'

'Oh yes, that's interesting.'

'But she doesn't write like I speak, if you know what I mean . . .'

'Oh, you mean sort of poetry . . .' said Mary.

'Yeah, that's right, poetry.'

126

'Why don't you bring some along?' said Mary. 'I'd love to see it.'

When they met, Mary had recognised Jan as the woman she used to see, around the corner from her own house, collecting a child being dropped off by a special bus, and carrying her into the house. She thought then that that must be some undertaking. Amazing how they had circled around one another within the same few miles, never quite meeting.

Jan had brought Paula's words.

'Brilliant,' said Mary, to Paula. Jan noticed this. It was extremely rare for anyone to address a remark to Paula. Usually they spoke about her, above her head, through a third person. She instantly warmed to this smiling woman with the cloud of curly blonde hair.

Mary and Jo read the words.

> Sometimes I'm happy, Sometimes I'm sad
> Sometimes I'm lonely, Sometimes I'm glad
> But as long as I have you
> I'll always love you

Jo took the four lines to the piano. A tune came into her head immediately and within three minutes she played Paula's song back to her.

'These are beautiful words,' she said, 'but it's only four lines. Would it be possible for you to write four more so that I could write a proper song?'

A week later Paula, assisted by Lois, the head pointer and an electronic typewriter, having devoted every hour of every day that she had the strength for to the poetry, was back with the new verses.

> For as long as I have your love
> I can see good and I can see fun
> Free from trouble, free from harm
> For take the sun and take the moon
> You will always have my love
> Which will go, on and on, Mum
> A day without you is lost
> And pointless to live
> So I will gladly say goodbye.

It was only a matter of time. 'What are you doing tonight, Jan?' Mary asked on a subsequent Wednesday.

Jan, who was intending to play bingo, said, 'Nothing, why?'

'Would you stay and do something for us?'

'Yeah,' said Jan, hooked.

Thames Television were in the process of making a documentary, part of their series *Another Side of London*, featuring Chicken Shed. It was called 'A Place of Our Own'. They filmed it during May, showing a working session at Vita et Pax and at Mary's house. The camera lingered on Paula, seated at the piano beside Jo who played 'Sometimes', the music recurring throughout the film. There were close-ups of Jan and Eddie smiling proudly.

For Chicken Shed it was a not-to-be-missed opportunity, while their work was on show, to talk about money. 'Chicken Shed,' said Mary, 'is like the baby that has grown into a teenager and has all the growing pains a teenager has. We started small, with all the administration done in my house. Now we are very large and all the administration is still done in my house. The teenager, Chicken Shed, is running away with us, and we're desperately trying to hold on to the reins.' It was a plea for a theatre, a place to work and develop that work with the best possible facilities to create the highest standards. That way they could open the doors to people for whom doors had never opened.

From first walking through Chicken Shed's doors in April 1988, Paula and Jan (and soon afterwards Eddie) were, by May, sufficiently part of the Chicken Shed experience to take part in a peak-time London television item, broadcast in June.

Jo's immediate bond with Paula was reminiscent of Jo's meeting with Mary fourteen years earlier, when only three months elapsed between first encounter and first production. Mary and Jo both, in fact, had picked up on that something special in Paula, and Jo recognised a flow of inspiration in Paula's poetry.

Jan, in turn, supertuned as she was to every signal concerning Paula, had known at once that here were people who could be vitally important to Paula and with whom she, Jan, could really communicate.

Paula, having gone her entire eighteen years

unable to communicate even the most basic signals beyond her immediate family, had now made an immediate connection with total strangers. And the other Chicken Shedders responded as Mary and Jo did.

'Everybody who was involved with Paula completely and totally believed in her, and accepted her,' says Jo, 'and everybody knew that the reason we weren't initially able to communicate with Paula was as much our problem as hers, and that we were going to have to sort it out. It was very much a joint effort from the beginning.

'And because she was so shocked at how everybody did *not* seem to have a problem with her, she herself put every ounce of effort into showing the communication she could show. So she probably made it easier for us than she's ever made it for other people before.

'Of course, what she was offering was more than anybody else gives. They don't normally come in and give us a poem! We don't ask for auditions here – but she did one, she proved it, so they were never in doubt of what she had to offer.'

As the weeks passed, Jan felt as if a sharp pain was lifting. The tightness across her shoulders and in her lungs was relaxing so that she could breathe smoothly, even take a deep breath. It was the pain of people not believing, and Mary and Jo had eased it away.

CHAPTER 12

To Mary

A favourite, a rare someone
fallen from a yew
My message to Mary is
Go, see, feel my fast great
Seed of life. For we must
Go take the story so far

In September 1988, Paula's world – which in a few short months had changed beyond recognition, and which now held so much promise – was shaken.

Mary was told she had cancer. Nothing is ever out of the blue: she had been ignoring the warning signs for over a year, intending to seek medical advice. She had never once suspected it was cancer, telling herself that her bad health was due to a combination of things – pressure of work (both teaching and Chicken Shed), stress, and especially her profound grief at the death, after a short illness, of her beloved mother Dot.

But before the severity of her condition could be judged, she had to be admitted to hospital for exploratory tests. Chicken Shed were working on *Love of the Seven Dolls*, a significant fundraising production booked into the Piccadilly Theatre for October. Could hospital possibly wait a month? she asked. 'Better not,' said the doctor, but she was admitted to hospital the day after *Seven Dolls* had been rapturously received by its audience.

The result of the test was bad news, and Mary was undergoing radiotherapy within a week to contain the tumour and hopefully reduce it prior to surgery. Throughout the radiotherapy, Mary determinedly kept working and Jo and John repressed any fears they might have felt. Jo insists that she knew all along that Mary would recover; in any case, they made a commitment to take their lead from Mary: business, within reason, as usual.

With daily visits from her near and dear, Mary kept in touch with events, the office (powered by Wendy Shillinglaw) continuing to function in her house. Recuperating from surgery was different, however: Mary was totally out of action. Recounting this episode for the purpose of this book was the first time since her diagnosis that she had been able to talk about the experience without breaking down. It was a terrible time for her, the fear of the illness itself, believing she was going to die.

As shockwaves flooded through Chicken Shed, Paula became desperately frightened. To lose Mary, having just found her, was unthinkable. Paula needed constant reassurance. She wrote to Winnie Dacre for comfort and to have someone else allay her fears. She asked endless questions, but always, 'Is Mary going to die?' It was because of Paula's need to be comforted that Jan took the opposite view, because the alternative was too awful; but still Paula asked, 'Is it possible Mary might die?'

'Of course it's possible,' said Jan, 'but I don't think she will.' And she meant it, she felt it. Mary would come through this.

Together they visited Mary, in hospital and at home, having checked out first that they would be welcome. And Paula wrote a poem for her.

The day after Mary's cancer was diagnosed, Malcolm Heyworth, chairman of Chatsworth TV, took Mary and Jo out to lunch. He was a tried and trusted Chicken Shed supporter and ardent fan of their work. 'You're going to have a lot of time on your hands,' he told Mary. 'Write me a story that we can make into a West End musical which will be the essence of what you are.'

So they did. And it became three magical stories, *Gala*, *The Attraction* and *The King's Web*. Each was a reworking of the same theme, encompassing the Chicken Shed message: 'Look below the surface of people. When you are denied love and acceptance and respect, you weave webs around yourself, and those webs enclose you. Some kids in Chicken Shed . . . that's what has happened to them. Right from the beginning, they're told they can't do this, can't do that, and they start to believe it themselves; then they start not to be able to do it; then they start not behaving themselves, to be aggressive, and angry and the whole thing goes on, self-perpetuating.'

During Mary's illness, one of the projects Jo and John devised to keep her thinking positively was how best to reach children outside Chicken Shed – not as members, since they were already bursting at the seams – but so that they could learn and benefit from the Chicken Shed experience. This became an ongoing project. Out of these discussions, Jo had the idea that the best way to show children what Chicken Shed was about would be

135

to go into schools and set up workshops for the children.

But how to put this into practice? Gradually they devised a scheme whereby one mainstream school and one school for those with special needs would be brought together under the auspices of Chicken Shed, for Chicken Shed sessions. Then John said, 'Why only local schools? What about the whole of London?' So they wrote to thirty boroughs, and twenty-two elected to take part. This initial project culminated at the Royal Albert Hall, when 1000 children took part in *Anansi*, a Caribbean musical. The scheme took on a life of its own, with every school eager for it to continue. So was born Chicken Shed's Theatre in Inclusive Education course. Paula is a member of that team. And the scheme was subsequently extended from primary school to Enfield College of Further Education.

Because Mary looks back on her illness as a time when she was devoid of strength and energy, a sad and empty time, it is worth noting how fertile it actually was in the greater scheme of things. It was also during her illness that she grew closer to Jan, which was to effect a significant change in the lives of the Rees family.

In the meantime, though, it was a year before Mary was well again. After this, in October 1989, she received the national Unsung Hero Award in recognition of Chicken Shed's work.

Over the Christmas of 1989 Paula wrote a song dedicated to Jo and Chicken Shed, calling it 'We

Need Each Other'. It became the Chicken Shed anthem.

> Every person has to be dead
> Who does not believe in someone
>
> I believe in you
> I want everyone to be happy
> Like I'm happy with you
>
> I want everyone to be beautiful
> Like you're beautiful to me
>
> I play around
> And you still stay with me
> I stay out late
> And you keep wanting me
> Keep doing bad things
> And you go on loving me
>
> We need other
> We need each other, like songs need words

CHAPTER 13

Hot Kerri

Hot Kerri likes going to stunning sexy joy
Open up real hell going through your mirror
She tells cerebral palsy stand for your rights
Because she moved around
Don't stay if you mean
Half my body
Stop giving staring people
Just smile to be direct
To say what life about
Roots mirror a life, good use
What time you have to find understanding
And trust

It was only natural that Jan's initial feeling would be gratitude for what Jo and Mary had made possible for Paula. Because of them, she had won through. After years of hitting her head against brick walls of disbelief, Jan was finally able to say, 'Paula is now herself.'

For their part, Jo and Mary had no idea of the full story, although Mary remembered seeing Jan with Paula, and thinking, 'What an undertaking, and what a strong, gutsy woman that is.' And since Jan had always nursed her grief privately, it was never discussed.

As Jo's working partnership with Paula moved excitingly on, Mary slipped into the role of second mother. Paula actually called her that. 'I would probably be jealous of Mary if I didn't love her so much,' Jan once told me, referring to the special bond between Mary and Paula.

Life was changing dramatically for the Rees family. Within weeks of walking through the doors of Vita et Pax, they had appeared in a television documentary. Within months of that event they were busily involved in Chicken Shed's production, *Love of the Seven Dolls*. Jan and Eddie, who had never set foot in a theatre in all their lives, moved with consummate ease backstage, and mingled with the VIP audience at the after-show party.

There was also a new circle of genuine friends. This was proven when the gale-force winds of the storms of February 1989 scooped up the precious family caravan from its permanent site in Clacton, and dropped it, some distance away, in pieces, thus proving Jan's theory that 'just as things start to pick up God snaps His fingers and says "Here's something to worry about, Jan"', though how she equates divine intervention with her non-belief is one of Jan's endearing quirks. Jo happened to telephone the morning Jan had just heard the news. 'You sound a bit low, Jan, anything wrong?'

'You could say that,' said Jan. And told her. The caravan was their pride and joy, and had a special meaning for her: it was her safe haven, her escape. It was all that, and money written off; the insurance wouldn't cover it.

Within days, Jo had organised a benefit gig, and they experienced the Chicken Shed support system in action as Chicken Shedders donated favours (washing cars, aromatherapy, babysitting), raised £3000 and managed to instal the Rees family into another caravan in time for Easter.

Mary had always admired Jan for being brave and keeping the family close despite her hardships, and being such a good, strong, resourceful mother. Then, when Jan visited her during her illness, not often, never staying very long, always telephoning first to be sure of doing the right thing, she discovered another side to Jan, gentle, noncombative, sensitive. She noticed too, how unsettled Jan had seemed after the October production, going from the elation of the show and then suddenly crashing down to earth as life returned to daily normality. Mary saw how confining Jan's life was – that she was a highly intelligent woman who had devoted her life to her family without ever a thought to her own needs.

Very gradually they began to talk about personal things. Mary is a good, nonjudgemental listener, and bit by bit Jan confided, making Mary part of her struggle. Mary had become the friend Jan needed, the someone to talk to.

And it was, in the event, Jan's suggestion that Mary – by now fully restored to health – should do a play based on Paula's life. 'Then I can tell you the whole story.'

Mary resisted for a time. She could accept the pressure of listening therapeutically; she could see it was helpful for Jan. But she wasn't sure about the pressure of trying to put the story into a play; she wasn't a writer, nor was she certain it would be right for Chicken Shed or where it might lead.

She nevertheless allowed herself to be coerced, and eventually their talks began at Jo's house, where she, Jan and Paula could speak without interruptions.

The talks drew them closer. Sometimes it would be too painful for Paula; she would make a fuss and have to go out of the room. Some of the things Jan spoke about made Mary cry. It was a long, slow, painful process. Jan talked and Mary painstakingly wrote it all down.

Yet Mary still hadn't committed herself to a play. Mary's tendency to worry and her perfectionism are legendary, so one can only conjecture what mental convolutions she went through before agreeing to try to write a play, not to mention the hours spent writing it. And then the big worry: who was to play the parts of Jan and Paula? 'Who would you like?' she asked them, and they chose their own people – Louise Perry as Jan and Michelle Manzi as Kerri, with Paula herself an enigmatic figure on stage, watching her life unfold. After the first performance, Eddie and Ian, who had up till now wanted definitely to be kept out of it, asked to be included and parts were written in.

Even now, after several public performances on stages as diverse as a school hall with an audience of fourteen-year-olds, to one in London's West End facing a celebrity house, Jan finds it hard to explain her feelings while watching the play.

'I wanted it to be told because I was proud of what Paula had achieved, for other parents who might have someone like Paula, for doctors and teachers. But I didn't want to be recognised. I wanted to be a ghost in the background.

'I wanted to watch it alone. I used to think all the people in the theatre were watching me, watching myself on stage. At Chicken Shed, it was particularly upsetting, everybody knows us, I cannot be anonymous. In the West End, I could be just another person in the audience. I cried and it was a relief. Afterwards I could hide in the ladies' cloak-room until the rest had gone home.'

The play had and has a powerful impact on its audience. It also had a cathartic effect on the family, enabling them for the first time to examine and discuss their feelings and emotions with each other. After he saw the play for the first time, Eddie said to Jan: 'I didn't know. You should have told me. You never talked about it.'

'There wasn't anyone to talk to,' said Jan.

'There's always someone,' he said.

During 1994, the year *Paula: The Story So Far* was performed in the West End, Jan wrote Mary a letter which Mary has cherished. It came to light when I was sifting through photographs and both women agreed to its publication.

Dear Mary,

As you know it is hard for me to write down my feelings. My spelling and dictionary are appalling, but I just feel I have to say this to you and it is hard for me as this is the first letter I have written like this but you know my faults and I don't feel embarrassed writing to you.

We have known each other for six years now, and have I hope a close relationship. The support you have given me since I have known you, and of course Jo, has been that it has changed me completely. I have so much more confidence and when I get really down and upset before I had no one to talk to but now just knowing you are there gives me such comfort and support.

All my life Paula has always been my rose and I have always felt I haven't done enough for her, but now since knowing you my lovely rose has blossomed into a beautiful bush with so many branches reaching out and giving people so much. And without you and Jo I would never have known this. So may I say thank you and I love you.

Jan

I'm not going to rewrite this or correct it because I know it won't affect what I'm trying to say.

CHAPTER 14

The ballroom

Feel the ballroom marvel
Dancing face, dancing feet
Love from friends
Love from foes
Just fancy free and
People live for time

Fill all days with movie magic
Diamonds, dancers and daggers
Beautiful dresses, handsome men
Dreamy till the end

See love, danger and despair
Of everyone on the screen

When powerful people decide to do something, they certainly get things done. It is interesting to chart the progress directly from the evening of 13 March 1988. Through Lady Rayne, her sister, Lady Annabel Goldsmith, attended Chicken Shed's first fundraising gala at Sadler's Wells in December 1989. She in turn talked about Chicken Shed to the Princess of Wales, who attended their first Royal Gala, *Anansi*, at Sadler's Wells in October 1990 and indicated that she would be interested in becoming their patron. Her presence guaranteed news interest, and she subsequently attended events each year until her personal problems curtailed her public engagements.

But by this time she had put Chicken Shed on the front page of every newspaper, most notably when her attendance at a Chicken Shed production was the first official engagement after the announcement, in the House of Commons, of her separation from Prince Charles; and later, when she was photographed leaving a Chicken Shed gala in tears.

At one stage, Chicken Shed had Lord Palumbo, former chairman of the Arts Council, as chairman, Lady Rayne as president and Princess Diana as patron. Many supported Chicken Shed initially because of the royal connection, but whatever the initial lure it won hearts.

People get hooked on the Chicken Shed experience. The acquaintance who introduced me (impresario Jonathan Shalit) wrote the following:

'It must have been four years ago when I was asked by my grandmother Mrs Henny Gestetner, who was eighty-four, to be her date to an amateur theatre show. I asked her driver when he picked me up what time I would be free – this was half six. He said midnight. When I asked what we were going to see, he said he understood it to be a performance by handicapped (! a word *not* in the Chicken Shed vocabulary) children. Five and a half hours, which I dreaded. I entered the Empire, Leicester Square – full of glamorous people, many famous. The Princess of Wales came in. Trevor Nunn came on stage and introduced the programme of music and dance we were about to see.

'From that moment I was transfixed by the power of the stage performance and also I had encountered the most remarkable, compelling, selfless group of people I have ever met. It might sound corny to say this – but through having met Mary, Jo and Chicken Shed I think I am a better person. They set an example I can only aim to follow. I think this applies to many people who become involved with them.'

The limelight cast on Chicken Shed by Princess Diana attracted the attention of Michael Parker, arranger of the fiftieth anniversary VE Day celebrations on behalf of the royal family. He invited the company to take part in *Joy to the World* at the Albert Hall, which was televised, and noted the standing ovation for them. When the time came in May 1995 to celebrate VE Day, he devised the spectacular 'Heads of State' ceremony around 108 Chicken Shed members, two children leading each head of state, member of parliament and member of the House of Lords to sign an olive branch. The television commentator said: 'The Chicken Shed children are making a genuine impact on world peace.'

Among Princess Diana's friends and acquaintances was the late Countess Rothermere, wife of Lord Rothermere, proprietor of the *Daily Mail*. After attending a Royal Gala, she suggested Chicken Shed would be a good subject for a piece in one of the sister newspapers, and the resulting full-page feature by journalist Matthew Norman, in the *Mail on Sunday*, was the company's first major in-depth story in a national newspaper, reaching several million readers.

When Lady Rothermere died in 1992, Lord Rothermere requested that Chicken Shed sing at her memorial service. One of the congregation, Nicholas Coleridge, editorial director of Condé Nast, was so deeply moved by their music that when asked by Peter Palumbo for support in sponsoring a photographic exhibition in aid of Chicken Shed, it was a foregone conclusion that he would agree. The resulting *Vogue*-mounted exhibition, 'A Positive View', raised £150,000 in September 1994 towards Chicken Shed's building fund.

Meanwhile, Lady Rayne had involved her friend
Sir Harry Djanogly, a wealthy and generous ben-
efactor, low profile and indefatigable supporter of
worthy causes. Her description of Chicken Shed
was sufficient to catch his attention; he went to a
performance and, by his own admission, was 'immediately caught in the spell. One couldn't help but
wonder where would these young people be, but for
Chicken Shed – and the talent, the energy, the
enthusiasm was an inspiration.'

He invited his friend Norma Major to see the company in action, confident she would react as he had
done. She confessed herself to be 'overwhelmed'. In
the meantime, in October 1994, she hosted a lunch at
Chequers for 120 people, which raised £250,000
(Mencap, the charity with which Mrs Major has been
involved for several years, also benefited).

Princess Diana's high profile was, and has
remained, the excuse for some people to say: 'If
you've got Princess Di, you don't need any other
help.' Mary had no patience with what she calls
sanctimonious claptrap of the 'you should have done
it alone' genre. 'We were alone for many years; very
few people had heard of us. The minute Lady Rayne
became involved, or Pauline Collins said, "More
people should hear about this", and we started
going out into the public, that's when we started to
be noticed and that's how we built a theatre . . . or
rather, Lady Rayne and her friends built the theatre for us.

'We needed money for the theatre, and the theatre to get our work established and to move forward

from that. The fact that we now have to convince
people that this doesn't mean we have a lot of money
is another matter.'

In September of 1989, the *Enfield Gazette*
reported that Chicken Shed was finally to be given a
home: Broomfield House, a 16th-century burned-
out mansion in Palmers Green . . . and £80,000 was
coming from the council towards its restoration. In
October 1990 the council pulled out of the project,
despite having agreed in the interim to increase its
stake to £2 million (financed by securing local spon-
sorship), conditional on Chicken Shed raising £1.8
million. Chicken Shed had so far raised £250,000;
the council, nothing. The council (unanimous
throughout in its goodwill and support of Chicken
Shed) was reported as saying it had bowed to pressure from English Heritage, who saw the theatre as
detrimental to Broomfield House. Mary stamped
her foot and said what was she supposed to tell
Princess Diana.

So the council gave Chicken Shed part of its
Bramley Road sportsground at Cockfosters, and at
a cost of £1.3 million (raised by Lady Rayne's committee) the New Theatre opened in December 1994.

In March 1996 it was reported that a restaurant
chain was to take over Broomfield House. The council had to decide between Harvester and Fork and
Pitcher.

CHAPTER 15

Mad little sad boy

A mad little sad boy
A dance with you is worth two
A lot of fun and a lot of sun
A seaside lover on the run

For good and for bad the sun will shine
For love and for hate the moon will shine
A little love is all we need
To make the day go by

For sitting and sighing at all that is bad
For sitting and looking at all that is sad
A great time is all we need
To make the world go round

As we have seen, among the many eminent people in the theatre world who fell under the Chicken Shed spell was Trevor Nunn. He contacted them after seeing *The Attraction* at the Shaw Theatre in November 1990. The work deserved to be seen by a much wider audience, he said. They must tour. And he suggested they went to the Arts Council to ask for the money to do it.

It was the first project for which they had ever asked for funding. Unwittingly, they were about to jump into the lion's den.

The Arts Council advised them to put on a show which would showcase the piece, and invite, among others, the Arts Council and managers of possible out-of-town theatres to be included in a tour.

Which Chicken Shed did. But they were quite unprepared for the barrage of criticism and personal insults which followed. They had in effect been picketed.

The incident bore the hallmarks of a planned attack. People left their seats (noisily) during the performance. Then, at the following get-together arranged for discussion, Mary was suddenly dragged into a bitter argument. Having set up this

157

meeting with people who were going to support Chicken Shed's work – or so they innocently believed – they found themselves the target of vicious criticism.

Their 'supporters' had come deliberately armed and ready to knock them down. It was sad and upsetting. The bemused out-of-town theatre promoters watched and listened, aghast – any enthusiasm for what they had seen was immediately clouded by the prospect of becoming embroiled in controversy. Thus began Chicken Shed's conflict with the disability movement.

The theatre critic of *Dail (Disability Arts in London) Magazine* left readers in no doubt about what her estimation was of *The Night Before Christmas*. She referred to her 'misfortune to be present' and talked of 'the most bloated of casts (80 people) . . . Everyone was smiling, everything was heartwarming. And where were the disabled people? . . . dragged hither and yon by their non-disabled minders or placed on stage to act as . . . living breathing props . . .'

Mary responded by writing to the editor, more in sorrow than in anger.

The cast was . . . actually more 'bloated' than [the critic] suggests – there were 270 members of the cast, all of whom took part on the first and last nights and in two other performances on a rota system. There were therefore never less than 120 performers. The reason for this is the importance we place on performance as a means of education and of that basic element of our work, the development of the self-worth of every individual.

We are asked where were the disabled people. There are no disabled people in our company . . . others hold their own views on the rights of people to be categorised and I would not want to deny them those rights. Most people who belong to Chicken Shed do not wish to be labelled and therefore I cannot answer this question nor quote any statistics without first accepting the categorising of people and this I will not do.

. . . the description of some of our performers as living breathing props caused great distress to those performers and their families who felt it referred to them. I am sure on reflection [your critic] would agree that it was an unfortunate phrase to use . . .

Paula's sister Kerri then waded in.

I am writing concerning your article, 'They're Chicken' . . . I am the sister of Paula Rees, one of your so-called 'breathing props'. I asked Paula if she would like to write to you about your article and she wrote, 'I have no answers for people like that.' Her answer did not surprise me because over the last twenty years she has come across so many people who have knocked her as you have, that she can't be bothered to prove herself any more. However I found a poem that she wrote last year which we both feel would benefit you to read.

> Do not let the anger and the sadness of the
>   people make you different
> Say you will always stay the same
> Forever knowing, forever believing
>
> We are the losers in the game
> And if we don't say what we feel
> No one will know how laughing can seal
> So let them read of sadness and joy
> For hope will win again as long as there is
>   hope

I would just like to add that in my opinion you obviously know very little about Chicken Shed or their very worthwhile work. They are striving towards being a theatre company which advocates total integration. They do not claim to be perfect. But at least they are trying.

> Yours sincerely,
> Kerri Brown

Most Chicken Shed productions receive favourable reviews, some euphoric. So it had come as a surprise to find themselves at odds with the disability organisations.

Their first clash with the establishment was the inevitable result of their divergence from the norm, and of their insistence that people within Chicken Shed were capable of integration but the moment they left they were back to whatever was available for them outside, which is to be treated as an oddity, a disabled person, and to be kept separate.

But then to find that there was also opposition from disabled individuals was a major hurdle, and it happened when they became organised enough, big enough, and confident enough to go for public funding.

Originally, they applied to Greater London Arts (then part of the Greater London Council), and were always turned down, but they could never really understand why. No reason was given, and none was obligatory. In such circumstances the reasons can be legion. It could be that there isn't enough money, or that the applicant doesn't have the right project, or that the management structure isn't quite right.

When Chicken Shed started to put its head above the parapet, when the publicity was rolling, when Judi Dench, Michael Williams, Pauline Collins and John Alderton got involved, people started to take notice.

'We became involved with the Arts Council itself,' says Mary, 'and it was at that point that the opposition to us became vocal and showed itself. And that opposition is undoubtedly based on the worry that any money that went to us would therefore be taken away from them.

'Basically, the disability group believe that separatism is the way to effect change. By sticking together you remain stronger, by diluting you undermine the cause.

'The disability movement is made up of people

in their twenties and thirties who are bitter because of the way they have been treated by society, and rightfully so. Right from the beginning they have had the kinds of experiences we are talking about. They are angry, and the basis of everything they do is anger. Their view is that, if you are putting on a production and you have a disabled producer, a disabled director, a disabled lighting designer, a disabled whatever, by proving to society that the disabled are able to produce the same worth of work as the able-bodied, that is the way you achieve respect.

'It is a valid argument, certainly in the short term. In the long term it doesn't really go anywhere. If you start saying you're only going to have disabled people working on that, then are you only going to have blind productions, and deaf productions? And some people would argue yes. Then are you going on to say people who don't read? (They would call them people with learning difficulties.)'

(When Mary said this I was reminded of a story John Bull told me. When someone said to him that mentally handicapped people liked to be called people with learning difficulties, he said, 'Well, actually, they'd prefer to be called by their names.')

According to Chicken Shed, the Arts Council and all the funding institutions in the country have chosen the separatist viewpoint. They have chosen to fund groups who are separate, as opposed to any group that brings a variety of people together. Chicken Shed therefore do not fit in, and in funding terms represent a threat. Yet Chicken Shed have as members more people with disabilities than any other individual group and probably most groups put together.

At the time of writing, nothing is resolved. Mary remains optimistic. She quotes Martin Luther King: 'There will never be progress while society is in monologue. You have to have dialogue.'

Meanwhile Chicken Shed's cuttings book bulges with ecstatic notices: 'The degree to which this wonderful idea has been pursued is a profound example to us all. It deserves our greatest possible support and if we fail to become involved, we shall become losers.' Lord Attenborough

'Wonderful, warm-hearted, full of life . . . Chicken Shed's work is remarkable.' Janet Suzman

'It is not just their energy, stagecraft and the sheer enthusiasm of their performances, there is something much more profound. Their sense of commitment to an ideal of mutually dependent democratic theatre is remarkable.' *The Stage*

'Once in a while a breath of fresh air sweeps through the performing arts. But hopefully a north London group will have transformed that breath into a zephyr when their national tour comes to an end . . . proof that industry, enthusiasm and talent can be truly inspirational when expertly harnessed.' *Yorkshire Evening Post*

'Quite simply a visual experience not to be missed.'
Western Daily Press

And still the sour note. *Disability Now*'s television
critic took a swipe at the company's appearance on
the Laurence Olivier Awards. 'Let me introduce . . .
the Poultry Company . . . this group of non-disabled
and disabled performers . . . performed a customar-
ily emotive song called 'We Need Each Other' . . . I
don't know about needing each other, but it strikes
me that Chicken Shed needs disabled people for its
existence, only to deny them equality.'

This drew at least one stinging letter to the editor.
Susan Hill, Chicken Shed mother, took it up with
the critic, who wrote back to explain his remarks.

I write as someone who has had cerebral palsy
for my lifetime of 50 years. From that perspec-
tive, I view the world (and in my TV column,
what appears on the small screen) from the
starting point that disability is not a negative
state of affairs, but a positive one. In my opinion, and that of many others, our physical or
mental states are nothing to deny, and any
stigma originates from the rest of society. In my
case I am disabled by social attitudes and
behaviour and environmental barriers, not by
having CP. I don't want to turn away from the
term 'disabled people' because I prefer to think
of people such as myself and your daughter as
part of a community, united in striving for
social justice through civil rights, accessible

transport etc. Through my work in journalism and in television, I do what I can to contribute to the progress of the disability movement.

I don't think that such a movement would exist if every disabled person classed themselves first and foremost as an individual. I don't know whether anyone in the movement would discount individuality, but many like myself would say that it is secondary to being part of a solidarity movement. Quite simply, individuality divides. Unification provides strength. I care and have great empathy for people such as your daughter, in fact all your daughters, but I'm afraid that the world will not be changed through songs or performances that do not reflect the positive experience of disability, no matter how strong the messages are. Action comes through belonging to organisations which further progress outside this membership, not purely for those who are inside.

Now perhaps you will see the roots of my disagreement with your philosophy and that of Chicken Shed.

CHAPTER 16

A poem for Meatloaf

Dear Meatloaf

Feel cold, free from feeling cold
Crying so we are striding
To freedom
Life wonders, finds love
Until people try to find

Keep trying to free your life
Find your keeping do

Love Paula

If there is one phrase Jan likes to drop into the conversation, it is 'my daughter Paula, who is artist in residence at Chicken Shed Theatre Company.'

Since her appointment to the job, Paula attends Chicken Shed every day, unless illness prevents her – writing, going out to the schools with the Theatre in Inclusive Education project and in class with the BTec students of drama and the performing arts.

Physically, there has been an improvement, insofar as Paula can almost control her right arm. The Team (as the full-time, salaried Chicken Shedders are known) can do anything for Paula that Jan and Eddie do, thus relieving their burden of responsibility. Not many actors would be prepared or required to act as nursemaid or minder to a colleague, but at Chicken Shed they take it on quite naturally.

She 'writes' using a wooden board made by Eddie that has painted on letters. Typewriter and head pointer have been discarded. When using the board, Paula's body and arm are supported by a helper – usually nervous in case they appear to anticipate her next letter.

Jan is sometimes on the receiving end of Paula's

scorn. She didn't, for instance, understand 'altruistic', in a letter Paula was writing to Mary. And Jan is frequently exasperated by her daughter's writing habits, either by the interminable time it takes or by the suspicion that Paula might be slacking off. 'Come on, just get on and finish it,' she'll urge, and receive Paula's acid put-down: 'You're just a typical showbiz mother.'

Some mysterious process feeds Paula's imagination. Writing lyrics for *A Midsummer Night's Dream*, she came up with

> Will you fill a world after feeling
> Go ever my fairy –
> You free dreams
> We relive life
> From crying tears . . .

Jo Collins:

'Sometimes she communicates quite flippant things. Sometimes they are very deep observations about something to do with Chicken Shed. She sees herself as something of an agony aunt where Mary and I are concerned, especially if she thinks there is any friction between the two of us (not that there ever is real friction between us), and recently she wrote a few lines to us in which she included a phrase along the lines of "You and Mary have a unique love, you must never let it die." It was likely she had overheard a reference to perhaps a heated discussion or disagreement we might have had, which had been interpreted as a row.

'Recently, when Meatloaf was on the scene, Paula was working on a song which she hoped he would perform. She gave me the lyric and I said I'd work with it for a bit. This was a different situation because she was writing something which she hoped was in his style. I then had to write music in his style. This was a different process from her usual approach, this time with a little bit of commercialism coming into it. She had interpreted the kinds of words he would sing, now I had to interpret the type of music he would do.

'I listened to a few Meatloaf tapes to get me into it. Often she would ask me how it was coming along and I told her it was taking a bit longer than it usually would, and she got a bit worried. If the music doesn't come quickly when I sit at the piano, then I stop and try again later – it can take weeks. I've learned it is the best way for me. I think she thought I was trying to put her off, and I think she went through a bad stage with me of thinking maybe her lyric wasn't good enough and also if Meatloaf liked it I would start getting involved with him. It was jealousy of what she perceived to be my preoccupation with Meatloaf.

'It culminated in her writing down some of these thoughts, which she then showed me. We were together in the auditorium at the time, with Jan, who had been quite perturbed by Paula's moodiness for the past weeks, and had no idea what was at the root of it. Now it all fell into place.

'Paula felt she had offended me, there were apologies and tears and protestations.

171

'She is also remarkably skilful. She was asked to write a Christmas song and she did, very quickly, but the words were incredibly complicated and deep. After I'd read them, I phoned her and said: "This isn't what's wanted. It needs to be something more corny – for want of a better word – carols and mistletoe sort of thing." And the next day she came up with exactly that. Very commercial, written to a prescription. Only trouble was I couldn't find the music. She's quite happy to be advised or criticised. When she did the verse and the refrain "Perfect woman let's be forever", and I said it needs a catchy chorus that can come back in again and again and again, something about their relationship, summing that up, she did. "Come into my arms my darling". She's perfectly happy to have suggestions, but never try to change a word once she's written it.

'Sometimes I'll say to her can I change that word and she'll say no. And eventually she's right and she knows it. Even if I say, "It's very odd having those two words together, it's difficult to get any kind of rhythm. Can you change it?", she'll say no, so I have to go away and work around it.

'She's never actually said she doesn't like what I do, which sometimes worries me. I don't know myself whether it's going to be a slow ballad or rock and roll, until I sit at the piano playing with the words, and those words demand a melody and that melody then demands the mood. Sometimes when Paula has been writing for a show, I've set out to make one of her songs more lively to balance a surplus of pensive songs, and it never works. The

The original 'chicken shed', in Barnet, north London. (*Collections/Brian Shuel*)

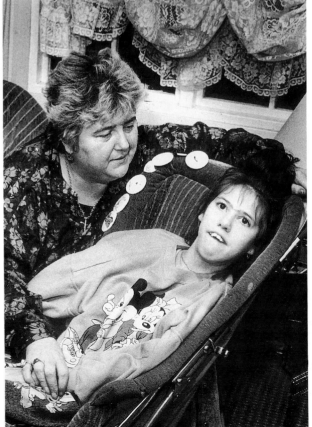

1988: Paula has just joined Chicken Shed and proudly displays the theatre company's badges on her wheelchair.

Exhilaration as Jo Collins plays her music and sings Paula's words, 'Sometimes'.

Paula's first experience of the very bright lights, *Love of the Seven Dolls* at the Piccadilly Theatre, 1988.

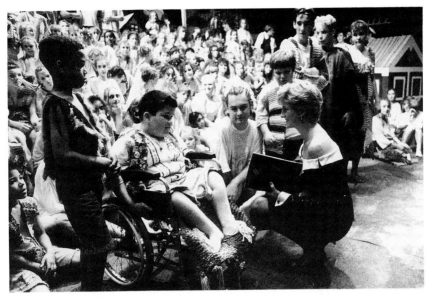

Chicken Shed's first Royal Gala at Sadler's Wells. After the performance of *Anansi* Princess Diana went on stage where the whole cast was assembled to meet her. Here she stops to talk to eleven-year-old Sean Walsh who had played a leading role. (*Brian Shuel*)

The Princess of Wales has a special word for Paula too. A friend on holiday spotted this picture in a foreign edition of *Hello!* magazine.

Children from Oakleigh Special School visit Livingstone School for joint art classes. Here seen working on ideas for *Anansi*, their sketches were subsequently used in Graham Hocking's set designs. (*Brian Shuel*)

A workshop at Bishop Douglas School. Mary Ward (right) and Christine Niering watch from the back. (*Brian Shuel*)

Mary at work with the group. (*Brian Shuel*)

When Paula's 'Song for Mum' was performed by Jo and played on radio, it brought the offer of a recording contract before the end of the show and made headlines in the local paper. (*London Standard*)

Chicken Shed had just achieved charity status and Judi Dench and Michael Williams were game to help with any photo opportunity for publicity's sake – just dip into the costume box . . . (*Brian Shuel*)

Lord and Lady Rayne were among the many supporters beating a path to Chicken Shed's door when the new theatre was up and running. This particular event, in November 1995, raised more than £20,000 for the new building.

Paula on stage as the Snow Queen in *The Night Before Christmas*, December 1992, positively shimmering in white tulle and feathers, sprinkled with sparkle. The costume was a gift from *Les Misérables*. (*Collections/Brian Shuel*)

Under the headline 'Isn't She Lovely?' the London *Evening Standard* ran this picture with a full-page story about Lissa Hermans on the day of the Royal Gala at the Equinox, Leicester Square, in November 1993. The event made news the following day too, with pictures of Princess Diana leaving in tears. (*Glenn Copus*)

A scene from the play *Paula: The Story So Far*. (*John Pridmore*)

July 1993: Jan, Paula and Sandy Gonzalez at Buckingham Palace to attend a garden party. Paula's outfit was a labour of love by talented Australian designer Tracy James, over on a visit at the time and helping out at Chicken Shed. The skirt is orange silk with an over-layer of matching chiffon, painted with splashy poppies. The material cost £70, a fortune in the Rees household but money well spent for the many times it has been worn – at every special occasion, including several Chicken Shed weddings!

Christine Niering and Brendan (left) on stage in *The King's Web* with Keiron Fay, September 1995. The production was being filmed for Chatsworth Television. (*Laraine Krantz*)

Jo sings 'We Need Each Other' – the unofficial Chicken Shed anthem – with Paula and the choir for the televised Olivier Awards, 1996. (*Laraine Krantz*)

words must demand their own treatment.

'We are not close friends, neither am I like a big sister to her. I've never had a similar relationship in my life; it's a very strong artistic relationship. I've had relationships with other musicians where you write together, but you tend to be offering the same sort of things. I've worked with other lyricists but there hasn't been that closeness, because they've worked conventionally, ABAB then the chorus, and it could be anybody's words.

'Paula is offering something completely unique coming from a completely different place. Also it is her sole means of communicating, it means so much to her, and it's a great responsibility resting on me. If one day I couldn't come up with the goods, she'd be very let down. She has so much faith in me, much more faith than I have. That faith often frightens me, Mary's faith in me frightens me, she always thinks I'm going to come up with something wonderful. She thinks I am infallible. I have a great belief in God, and I think that when I'm supposed to be writing I will, and when I'm not I won't be.

'It was clear early on that Paula's first poem wasn't just a fluke. As soon as she realised there were people who believed in her and someone who could actually interpret it in a musical way she wrote more and more. Even if poetry gets published, it reaches the smallest minority. Putting it to music makes it much more accessible, because people perform it. The most you get with a poem is a poetry reading. Take a song like "We need each other every person has to be dead who does not believe in someone" – you can hear that being read in some poetry reading somewhere, which is very heavy. Done to music and then danced, with "We need each other" done as a refrain, it isn't heavy at all.

'And then she just kept writing, wrote more and more. When we started to research *Paula: The Story So Far* we asked Jan if we could have everything Paula had ever written down and some of it was words in conversation, wise words such as "Do not let the anger and the sadness of the people make you different." It was just Paula speaking to her family. I made that into a song.

'Very occasionally she'll make a lighthearted remark, but mainly our relationship is very deep and meaningful and doesn't allow for trite comments. And never personal, unless it's about Mary and me. I don't open up to her either. Ours is a working relationship.

'I think initially Paula was definitely writing about all the years she was trapped, before she found this way of communicating and before people were prepared to believe it was her writing it and not somebody helping her. Something could happen now with the work, so it was worth all that effort. It was as if she had a backlog of things to say, so she wrote a lot over a very short period of time.

'Now, with her work at Chicken Shed as our writer in residence, she is commissioned to write, which she does. And with other musicians, which she is beginning to do, and that will be good for her, and for her development.'

There have been many people over the years at Chicken Shed who produce words, but only two who produce words which call from Jo the highest possible emotional output in terms of melodies. Paula, and Paul Morrall.

'We can all sit down and write words which come from our brain and heart and soul, but somewhere there is another ingredient that goes into Paul's words, Paula's words,' said Mary. Jo took up the thought. 'It is like a river, running, words flow down that river, and they reach me, and I write the melody and it returns to the river, a continuous journey . . .'

Paula and Paul could not be less similar. Paul has gone through the conventional system, has a degree, writes in metre and verse. Paula is the natural, has been taught nothing. He has no physical disability, she has enormous physical disability. Their work is of equal standard and calls the same sort of musical response from Jo.

'Sometimes,' said Jo, 'I don't want to talk about Paula's disability, I want to say, "Look at this poetry, doesn't it do something to you?" '

There was so much to learn about her, after that first meeting in April 1988.

CHAPTER 17

A Midsummer Night's Dream

Dream we real yew
We queen and goddess of beauty
Titania see live always free
And fairies move with
Unbelievable care
Fairies yew go far away
Years go by free from having
Your wish feel made

Dreams come with stories
God, me and fairies
Tell from dreams, lay stories
From leaping truth
Real wishes would fill
Wonders, for stories you find
for love

See your face will you fill a world after feelings
My fairy you free dreams
We relive life from crying tears
We want fading love to go
Yew fall if you want dreams
Leave see feel dreams may be far

Look along any Chicken Shed line-up – Shakespeare to junior jazz to a musical play – as they take their bow, brilliant performers, radiant smiles, and the hidden question is: what if there was no Chicken Shed? Whether it's a sweeping transformation (as happened with Paula and the Rees family) or a delicate, subtle contact which in passing plants a thought that lingers on, without doubt the Chicken Shed experience changes every life it touches.

Everyone always remembers Brendan. He is the charismatic young man of uncertain age (in fact twenty-six at the time of writing) with Down's syndrome whose personality fills the stage as he dances with joy, precision and authority, his face, and especially his eyes, holding his audience.

When Brendan was thirteen, he was taken along to a Wednesday youth theatre evening at Vita et Pax by staff from a nearby residential centre for mentally handicapped children, where he had been placed in care because his mother had died. He clearly enjoyed the session; he went several more times, and then he stopped. He had gone to live with his sister. Several weeks passed before

Wendy Shillinglaw (Mary's right hand, working at the office in Mary's house) received a phone call. It was Brendan's sister, relieved that she had finally tracked down this 'chicken' Brendan had been pestering her for. 'He kept saying chicken. I thought he meant he wanted it for his dinner,' she said. And so Brendan returned to Chicken Shed.

His partner in dance is choreographer Christine Niering, herself a Chicken Shed child, who finished university determined to become a choreographer and was drawn back to work for the company. She describes her relationship with Brendan:

'He has a natural stage presence, a natural, quite astounding understanding and knowledge of what he is being asked to do dramatically. Mary's relationship with him is very special, and he'll absorb her direction perfectly and produce exactly what she wants and more. And exactly the same with dance. He has an uncanny feeling for line, is very flexible, very strong, sensitive. So that coupled with his sense of drama makes him incredibly charismatic.

'As he walks into Chicken Shed, you can practically see him change. He comes in rather stooped, his shoulders hunched, his hair quite messy. A couple of minutes later his hair is brushed, his back straightens up, his eyes are bright, he's ready for work – if we're sitting around having coffee he is impatient to get started.

'Untainted by mundane day to day things which clog up the rest of us, Brendan's heart and mind are open to the work, that's why he manages to project

180

this incredible aura and power which everybody comments on whenever they see him work, whatever he is doing.

'So you dance with him . . . I'm quite a bit taller so when I partner him I have to keep my legs bent or work on the floor, but his eye contact is so strong . . . honest is the word that springs to mind because whatever he is doing, he will perform it with such honesty that it will enable you to click in to a better way of performing. It has taught me confidence.

'Like anybody, if he's had a bad day he might be distracted. More often than not he will reproduce again and again and again exactly the right level of performance that is called for, which is something for which most of us struggle. We have a good night and a bad night – Brendan has this way of producing the good night. It's his whole world I guess. It means everything to him.

'He's not held back by any inhibitions. He's very physical when he is dancing and he enjoys being physical. Understandably so, I don't expect he gets hugged very much and touched very much. For him dancing is very physically stimulating as well . . . his development of the way he communicates with people now is tied in with his ability to take in a high level of technique. Socially, too, the way he can now sit in with a group and listen. Before, he was so locked into his world he was incapable of sitting in and listening, he had to be doing something. It's brilliant too that he is able to work with people of such high standard, the mix is incredibly stimulating for him, and also for people

181

who want to understand him.

'I used to have a problem hearing people say how brilliant Brendan's dance was. I started to ask would they still think it was brilliant if Brendan wasn't Brendan? Yet I know his talent and his stage presence are indisputable.

'I distinctly remember the first time I saw Brendan on stage, many years ago, and thinking he had amazing stage presence.

'He was – is – quite small, and sometimes he has his head down, but it was something about his eyes, the sparkle, and his whole attentiveness. You could see he was loving what he was doing, he was communicating and he was allowing himself to be communicated to.

'Backstage he gets nervous like the rest of us. And when a show is finished, he is very let down, very quiet. He shed some tears the last night of *A Midsummer Night's Dream*, when the boys took him out to the cab which was driving him home.

'It is very sad to think of Brendan away from Chicken Shed. The month's summer break is especially hard for him; he comes back looking unhappy, unwell. You imagine him watching television all day, playing his Chicken Shed tapes over and over and over again.'

The evening that Christine Niering watched Brendan on stage at Sadler's Wells and was struck by his ability to engage his audience was Chicken Shed's first Royal Gala performance, in the presence of the Princess of Wales. Also in the audience was Sue Hill, a mother of three who had bought her tickets for *Anansi* with one specific purpose in mind – to check out what she had heard about Chicken Shed.

'I went to see the show with a view to looking for people with Down's syndrome on stage, and whether they could perform as well as the others. A friend had told me about Chicken Shed. She had a severely disabled child and had told me, "But I've found this place, amazing." So I wanted to see them in action.'

The curtain went up and she became engrossed in the show. It wasn't until the final curtain that she realised she hadn't identified anyone as having Down's syndrome because in her enjoyment, she had forgotten what she had come for!

She booked for their next date (*The Attraction* at the Shaw Theatre one month later) and meanwhile wrote to Mary Ward: 'For the last seven years I have tried to integrate my daughter into the mainstream. You've done it in one evening.'

Emma was born in November 1983. From early pregnancy, Sue Hill felt there was something wrong with the baby. There was a threatened miscarriage at seven weeks and at sixteen weeks she was so uneasy about the baby that the hospital carried out a scan to measure the baby's head and development, and pronounced all was well.

After the baby was born Sue learned that the child had Down's syndrome. She remembers the sound of herself screaming, the sight of her husband sitting in the corner of her room shaking his head in disbelief at her reaction and saying to the doctor, 'I thought she'd be OK.' She remembers thinking, 'I'm never going to smile again. This is the end of my life.'

Obliged to breastfeed her child who refused the bottle – the only alternative would have been to feed by tube – she couldn't bring herself to hold her daughter, nor even to look at her. 'All I could see was an empty shell.'

Eventually, on sufferance, she took her baby home, promising herself 'it would be only for a year, the best bit. A baby is a baby for its first year. After that I'll give it back to the hospital.' Within weeks her devotion was absolute.

When, at eight months, Emma was sitting up unaided and a visiting posse of paediatricians proceeded to spell out all the negative aspects she had to contend with regarding Emma's projected poor development, Sue's hackles began to rise and have remained thus for much of Emma's life.

When a well-meaning neighbour arranged for her to look over a nursery school for children with special needs, what Sue saw was a meeting place for mothers to chat over coffee while their babies lay on cushions on the floor or sat rocking to and fro. Later she visited another education unit for the mentally retarded where the lack of dignity extended to ever-open toilet doors; and a request from a student to hold Emma was turned down by kindly staff with 'Oh no, you'll drop her'.

Staking her claim by every device she knew (painting the school hall, cleaning the windows in the new library), Sue Hill ensured a place for Emma at the schools her older daughters Natalie and Kathryn attended. Once installed, Emma held her own.

By this time Sue Hill was accustomed to discrimination. When she wanted Emma to join the Brownies, Sue had to join also. 'We moved up to the Guides and I had to go camping, and go to the loo in the fields. I'd never done that in my life before. Emma was interested in joining a gym, so I had to join because they "couldn't accept responsibility" for her. She wanted to swim, I had to go to lessons with her, and into the pool alongside although I cannot swim at all and hate water. They told me children like Emma never learn to swim. In fact she swims like a fish. She was just being labelled.'

After Sue's letter to Mary Ward, Emma was welcomed to Chicken Shed. Sue wasn't obliged to attend but usually she did. For the first three months Emma sat in a corner, her head between her knees, refusing to chat. (Her sisters too were fairly shy.) Then she suddenly blossomed into a fully contributing member of the company, and has remained so ever since.

When it came to senior school, Sue Hill found herself up against the local education authority which challenged Emma's right to remain in mainstream education. It had been suggested that some staff would not be happy with a Down's syndrome child in the school, that Emma had special education needs and that to classify these needs Emma would have to be 'statemented', i.e. examined and assessed in a way not required for all pupils. What the headmaster saw as the means to provide additional support for Emma, Sue saw as reinforcing the practice of labelling special needs children.

'Every child has "special" needs in one way or another. Emma doesn't have any special support at Chicken Shed; she doesn't have special support at home; she hasn't needed special support at school. She is confident, she feels good about herself. Mainstream education is where she belongs.'

Tara and Tanya, dusky-skinned, silken-haired twin daughters of Zeeta Jacobs, were born in January 1988, around the time Paula was nearing eighteen and Jan was contemplating what sort of future Paula could hope for. Like Paula, they were born in Chase Farm Hospital.

Theirs was a traumatic birth, seriously premature. Zeeta had been in hospital for several days before being told her babies were dead and given medication to induce labour. Her insistence that she was sure the babies were still alive, that she could feel them moving, was dismissed.

The babies, barely a handful each (weighing two pounds eleven ounces in total), arrived. She remembers the expressions of surprise on the faces of medical staff when they realised the twins were actually alive, one breathing unaided, the other with difficulties. Their prospects were poor. In any case there was no ventilator available; or, rather, there was one but hospital policy decreed that, in the case of twins, they must not be separated. An emergency call went out, and two doctors and a nurse arrived to transfer the girls to hospital in Harlow, Essex.

Zeeta's husband (they are now divorced) went to the hospital in Harlow to see his daughters, and to name them Tara (Twin Number One) and Tanya. Zeeta had not known or considered the names before; and, anyway, the choice was academic since the twins were not expected to survive.

In shock, still bleeding, Zeeta shuffled around the wards, feeding small change into telephone units to call Harlow for news of her babies. Tara was given the last rites. Miraculously she clung on.

And it was that clinging on which touched a chord. While Tanya gradually picked up strength, began to lose the transparency of her skin and become a normal colour, to function like a baby should, Tara lurched from crisis to crisis: pneumonia, lung collapse, septicaemia, epileptic fits, inability to feed, chronic vomiting, blindness, and brain damage caused by oxygen deprivation at birth. She developed hydrocephalus (dangerous swelling of the head which used to be known as 'water on the brain') and contracted meningitis while still in hospital (certainly it could be said fate was loaded against her).

By the time she was three, Tara had spent most of her life in hospital. Twice doctors offered – suggested even – that the life-support machine should be turned off. Tara's life was not a real life, they said. Better she be allowed to slip peacefully away, now. Zeeta became accustomed to bad news. Tara, she was told, wouldn't survive the first year; she'll never have any quality of life; she'll be purely vegetative.

'I felt I was fighting for her,' Zeeta recalls. 'Whatever her condition I wanted her to stay alive. I had such intense feelings, she'd fought so hard. She did nothing, but I felt she knew I was there. She deserved me to fight for her. And there was Tanya, a twin, I was afraid she would never know her twin sister.'

Zeeta's marriage broke down under the strain. With her round-the-clock hospital visits, her older children, Roxanne (now eleven) and Lauren (seventeen), needed daily foster care. The twins were four before the family was able to live together again. Never out of danger, Tara needs constant medication and nursing, and has a gastrostomy, which means she is fed through a tube in her stomach, overnight, while she sleeps.

When a close friend suggested Zeeta's children joined Chicken Shed, she was aware of the need to brighten their lives and re-direct her own. Her marriage was already in its final crumbling stages.

It has surprised them all that, given the stimulation and motivation to shine, Tara can match her twin. From the bar where she helped out (before joining the production team), Zeeta could peep through the doorway at a rehearsal session and 'watch Tara being made to do something, what everyone else was being made to do, and after the initial "poor me" she did what she was told. As her mother I presumed because she is disabled and has only half a brain that she couldn't keep up; here she is expected to walk, talk, understand and follow direction. She plays a game . . . refusing for a while then performing, her attitude being "I'll do it because I want to". Her main disadvantage is being unwell more often than most, which we must accept.'

Her experience of mothering Tara has left her with an underlying bitterness at what she describes as 'so many things stacked up against us, not least the accepted view in medical and so-called caring services that a child with serious disability isn't going to have any quality of life, and that a mother who thinks otherwise just isn't coming to terms with reality.

'Many parents who have children born with disabilities are over-protective, it's natural, and easily conditioned to believe a normal quality of life is out of the question. "Half the brain is dead" – the assumption is that the child might as well be dead. A lot of parents will go into despair when constantly hearing that.

'I was always being told I was in denial, that I would only be able to come to terms with Tara's total disability when I learned to grieve for what she might have been.

'My fear was, would I be allowed to expect her to achieve?'

Her fervent wish, or as she describes it her dream, was always to find some other person, as disadvantaged as Tara, who had nevertheless achieved a quality of life. 'And then I met Paula and meeting her did something for my spirit. She epitomised quality of life, what she is mentally tells so much about that quality. I've learned to cope with my feelings.'

Jo Collins was finishing a session at Vita et Pax, had left the piano and was having a cup of tea, when she heard someone at the piano playing a song that she had taught that evening to accompany a dance, someone singing and sounding so very much like Jo herself as to be almost identical. She looked across at the piano. The pianist was a newcomer; Lissa Hermans, not yet eight, blind, so far totally uncommunicative, diagnosed autistic. Astonished, Jo went in search of Jane Hermans, Lissa's mother. Where and how did Lissa learn to play, who had taught her?

Jane replied that Lissa was encouraged to amuse herself playing on her grandfather's piano, 'and she sings along to records'. She added that she had been told by experts that this ability to copy sounds was part of the autism syndrome.

Jo asked Lissa to repeat the piece. She did, note for note a copy of Jo, same style of playing, the same inversions of chords. Uncanny, thought Jo, and she said so.

It was also extremely exciting, especially since Lissa was so young, and without wasting any time Jo began working with her. 'We gave her solos and she was brilliant. Not only could she copy on the piano, note for note, what she had just heard, she could hear a song and sing it all the way through, and know it perfectly. She just got better and better. A great voice, the sound, the tone, the range, the strength . . . and to have a voice like that at eight is even more extraordinary. A prodigy no less.'

Lissa was born on 23 October 1981. Within a few weeks Jane began to suspect that all was not well, that there was something wrong with the baby, something more than Lissa being just a particularly distressed, colicky baby; a serious problem. Voicing her misgivings, she found they were shared by her mother, and together they took Lissa to their GP to learn their instincts were depressingly well founded. Lissa was blind. Christmas Eve was spent having hospital tests; they were promised further details would follow, but from the outset there was never any hope of a cure.

Jane, her parents and Lissa's father spent Christmas in a state of shock. Jane and Lissa's dad had been together for a year 'but once we had the baby and she was colicky, up all night, and then blind as well, things weren't very good, and he left us when she was five months. And hasn't been in touch since.' Jane recounts events in a matter-of-fact way, not seeking sympathy, not speaking his name. 'I was relieved . . . I'd had two people to care for and now it was one, so I was better off, plus I had the support of my parents.'

As well as being blind (her type of blindness from birth is extremely rare), Lissa was diagnosed as having a rare pituitary condition causing growth deficiency. The word 'Panhypopituitarism' is printed on the bracelet she must wear at all times, a warning should she be taken ill that her pituitary gland isn't working fully and that she needs urgent medical help.

Hospital visits and admissions became a way of life; they still are. She was an uncommunicative little girl, unwilling or unable to connect, even with her mother and relatives. Because she couldn't see colours and picture books her mother instinctively gave her toys which created sound. It gradually became obvious that she didn't just bang things, she would make rhythmic sounds. Jane learned that if she wanted to catch Lissa's attention she had to sing rather than speak. Lissa was solitary, afraid of unfamiliar sounds and new or strange situations, didn't speak until she was three and thereafter rarely. Along with her natural fears, she developed phobias. One – her terror of any powder substances – has only just come under control as she has grown accustomed to stage make-up.

She always loved music. By the time she was seven, she could pick out a tune on the piano, could sing the entire score of a musical, yet still couldn't tell her mother what she needed; she could sort out her tapes by shaking them although she couldn't put on her shoes. Jane sought out situations, using music, which she thought would encourage Lissa to open up, and for a time Lissa attended Cheviots' music group, but always maintaining her own silent shell. And then Jane saw an item about Chicken Shed on *Blue Peter*, showing excerpts from their *Love of the Seven Dolls* at the Piccadilly Theatre. Immediately recognising the potential for Lissa, Jane rang for tickets but the show was sold out. She asked for a number, made contact with Wendy Shillinglaw, working at Mary's house, and Lissa's name was put on the Chicken Shed waiting list.

It seemed to Jane – for whom luck had so far not been evident – that to discover Chicken Shed was so close by was more than she could ever have hoped for, that fate was finally on her side.

They were eventually invited to an open evening. That Lissa couldn't see was immaterial as far as Chicken Shed were concerned. More to the point was Lissa's insularity. A very clingy child, she sat hanging on to her mother throughout that first session, despite the boundless energy, friendliness and warm welcome she received. Even with sight she could have been reticent, as many children are; but her blindness increased her fear of unfamiliar sounds and sensations.

'Then Wendy said "I have just the right person for Lissa," ' says Jane, recalling their first visit, 'and introduced Michelle Manzi, one of Chicken Shed's education team, who from that evening always sat beside us. And gradually, over a few weeks, Lissa let Michelle touch her hand.'

Little by little, with this gentle encouragement, Lissa began to relax and to indicate that she enjoyed the sound of the singing. And then came the evening she got up from her seat and crossed the room to play the piano and demonstrate her remarkable voice.

Once Jo realised just how remarkable Lissa was, she determined that Lissa should have a keyboard at home. An approach was made to Cassio by Dave Carey, one of the music team and a contributor to the magazine *Keyboard Player*, who thus had good connections in the business.

Generously, Cassio agreed to donate a keyboard. Could a celebrity be found to make the presentation? Stevie Wonder was appearing on stage at Wembley; would he co-operate? Word came back (Wembley press office liked the idea, a great picture opportunity): yes and no. He wouldn't present the keyboard, but he would be delighted to meet Lissa, and a date was fixed.

Dave Carey, Jane and Michelle escorted Lissa to Wembley and backstage to the star's dressing room. It is fair to say that Lissa was the only one not impressed by the privilege on offer; she hadn't even heard of Stevie Wonder, and kept proclaiming 'I don't want to meet Stevie Wonder, I don't want to meet Stevie Wonder . . .' right up to the moment when, surrounded by a bevy of minders and assistants, he stood before her, with a welcoming smile and hand outstretched.

One of Lissa's behavioural quirks at that time was a door fixation. She had found a door she wanted to swing to and fro, and Jane and Michelle were intent on preventing her. Stevie Wonder found this very amusing, and when he laughed she stopped struggling to get out of Michelle's lap and to the door, but continued to cry.

The star moved away to the other side of the room, to his keyboard, and began to play a few notes to distract her. She stopped crying and walked towards the sound, joining him at his keyboard, cheekily knocking his hands off. He listened then played the same phrase – backwards. The game began, a musical conversation between the two of them.

Then he said: 'Lissa, do you like this keyboard?'

'Yes.'

'Then I want you to have it.' And she hugged him. Stevie Wonder's keyboard is with Chicken Shed; the excellent Cassio meanwhile is perfect for Lissa's home needs.

There was a postscript. A Dutch film company making a documentary about Stevie Wonder heard from him of 'this amazing kid' he had met in England. They traced Lissa to Chicken Shed and filmed an interview with her and Jo at Jo's house.

Throughout, Lissa was totally unco-operative, her nose buried in a book. As the cameramen were packing the lights away, Jo said to Lissa: 'I should have taught you "You Are the Sunshine of My Life", since this is a programme about Stevie Wonder.' And began playing it. Inevitably Lissa joined in, providing the director with the shot he wanted. The crew unpacked their equipment and began shooting all over again. The hour-long film is continually being shown on television worldwide; its final scene shows Lissa singing, with Stevie Wonder's voice singing in the background, as the camera pans away from Jo's front door.

Today Lissa is an accomplished performer who brings an audience to its feet with applause. Jo assesses Lissa thus: 'She wasn't at that time an accomplished pianist but she knew what she wanted to play, she had the sound in her ear, she could find it and translate it. She is not unique, there are known cases of children who can just sit down at the piano and play without ever having had a lesson or the opportunity to tinker before.

'We read about these strangely gifted children – that doesn't make it any the less exciting when you actually meet this gift yourself.

'Lissa is highly musical, an epic musicologist. Perfect pitch is a phrase bandied about, and very few people have it. Basically it means opening your mouth, singing a note and saying, "That's a C." It's rarely right. I can't do it, I can get it roughly right. Lissa has got perfect pitch. I'll ask her, "How did that song go?", and she'll sing it exactly right, in the right key. I can play something in C and she'll sing along to it in C. Then I'll say, "How did I teach it to you?", and she'll sing it in D flat, a semi-tone higher, the key I originally taught it to her. That is extraordinary, a semi-tone is nothing, most people wouldn't hear the difference.'

Lissa is now learning the Suzuki method of playing the piano, whereby she is trained to use all her fingers instead of her preferred three, thus developing a technique for classical music.

What most pleased Jane was not Lissa's musical success but her daughter's new-found happiness. As her confidence grew she acquired the knack of relating to others and establishing friendships. 'At Chicken Shed, initially the problem was how sociable she was going to be. Given Lissa's personality, the fact that she is part of something is more amazing than the fact that she sings. By nature she is insular; people aren't very interesting to Lissa and she's not a great mixer. Now all of a sudden she had people around her, musical people, caring people, people who were willing to take her on face value.'

Gradually Jane stopped going to the sessions; Lissa needed space and so did she. Michelle became Lissa's support.

'She finds it very hard to say to me I'm very unhappy or I'm fed up and yet she can sing about emotions from the heart. And when she is singing she has an astonishing gift for interpretation, even emotional adult things which you would not imagine she could have the understanding for. Perhaps because she has this outlet to express emotion, she doesn't need to tell me about hers.

'We have a way of coping in our lives. Lissa has stories about everything that has happened in her life, and if she is stressed, I ask her which story she wants to hear, so that she can replay it in her head. I don't think they're particularly cheery stories, but the familiarity comforts her. She knows about the sadness. So I tell the stories – whom I spoke to, where we went. For Lissa the important features are the transport, who was there, what the room was like, what the bed was like (if it is a hospital story), small or big. She tries to picture herself in those situations.'

When Lissa joined Chicken Shed in 1988 the full impact of Paula's extraordinary gift was shining like a beacon. One of the first songs she sang when she began to open up and join in was Paula's 'Sometimes'.

'Her songs are quite sad, mostly, and emotional.

They're all beautiful,' Lissa says, adding, 'that all seems so far away' – probably a reference to all that has happened to her since.

She adores the thrill of being on stage. Speaking slowly, in measured tones, she explains: 'I feel the audience looking at me. I just stand there and sing, and listen and I have them with me.

'Jo tells me certain things to do, turn this way or that, I can sense what the audience can see.' She would like to make a career out of teaching singing, 'and earn some money and then I can buy Mum a house.'

Jane Hermans talks of sorting out her life now that Lissa seems settled. She has resumed working part time, and feels the benefit of having an outside interest. Her life has turned around since Lissa's discovery; one effect is that she has become a Christian.

'Having a blind child, a sick child, going through all that illness and all those problems made me angry. I was angry at God. I might have seemed strong on the outside, I was paying a high price inside. I had inner conflicts. And I was happy to be a martyr, I thought that was what I deserved. Then as Lissa developed, so did I. Before, I was constantly having to think of her, for her, create something around her, to make her happy and to break through that reserve.'

You imagine her living with this small child in a deafening silence. Now their relationship, she says, is so normal they actually bicker like all mothers and daughters.

Jane deliberately remains on the fringes of Lissa's Chicken Shed life, which was the culmination of her search for 'a place where Lissa wasn't going to be the Lissa I had known. This Lissa would have a life of her own. We both need our space.

'From the moment we came into Chicken Shed, Paula was an inspiration to us both. Jan, what she had achieved, was an inspiration to me. But hers was a harder task, she had to prove things; Lissa had only to be heard.'

CHAPTER 18

A song for Mary

I love the way you smile
I love the way you laugh
I love the way you have of asking me to stay
I love the way you dance
I love the way you play
I love the way you have of asking me to stay
I love the way you talk
I love the way you walk
I love the way you have of asking me to stay

I love the way you sing
I love the way you act
I love the way you have of asking me to stay

From Paula xxx

Mary was speaking of Paula. 'When Paula first came, I automatically assumed we could communicate because I always assume everyone can understand. I didn't go into the relationship with any other thought in my head – except that I knew she couldn't reply, so I didn't know how to receive communication from her. I just talked to her and assumed she understood, which was backed up by what Jan and Kerri said, and by what Paula wrote.

'Like the rest of us she has a thousand million ways of showing her feelings. It's impossible for us always to guess. Jan knows, as mothers know their own children, but unlike the rest of us who don't have a physical connection with our children after a certain age, Jan has gone on having that connection with her.

'Quite soon – probably within a year – I began to get communication from her. I watched Jan, I watched Kerri and I formed my own way.

'It is still difficult because she can't get up and follow me out of the room if she hasn't finished the conversation. Sometimes she may be cool towards you, and it could be because on the previous occasion you left before she'd finished. Perhaps she wanted you to go on a bit, say a bit more and you broke off the conversation before she was ready, and she might be harbouring resentment. Anybody else could say, "By the way, last time we were talking you cut me off before I had finished" . . . it's out in the open. Paula can't do that. A slight can become a barrier.

'Paula is a strong and highly confident character. Just because she happens to be in a wheelchair, there is the implication that she is the simple, straightforward, uncomplicated one of the two sisters, whereas the opposite is true. Kerri is the softer, highly flexible sister. Paula is highly complicated, highly intelligent, with not a nasty streak but with an edge. Kerri has no edge, she is an exceptionally nice person, a truly beautiful personality, much more easily crushed.

'Paula's heart is as big and soft as Kerri's, she has as much generosity in her, but a different personality. She cannot afford to waste words or time. Paula is still battle-scarred, and like Jan, has her own way of dealing with it.

'Her health fluctuates dramatically. Sometimes she has to take drugs to ease her pain, and the drugs have the effect of slowing her down, deadening her brain activity so that her brain, which is usually so sharp, is being sedated. That's another thing she battles against. Sometimes when she is dying to communicate, she can't because of the pain or the drugs or both.

'She can indicate the area of pain, but she cannot explain or describe it. After all, she has had pain all her life. We have several people like Paula in Chicken Shed, who have lived all their life in pain so that they don't know what it is not to have it.

'My relationship with Paula is quite different from Jan's, and quite different from what I imagine Jan thinks it to be. Sometimes it is very deep, very affectionate. Other times she can be quite cool with me. It is physical, I can feel it like a tension. Sometimes she is very soft and open, very glassy, her eyes seem transparent. Sometimes, if Paula is really communicating with you and is feeling loving towards you, her eyes become like lakes, you feel you're swimming in this beautiful lake, surrounded by warm water as if you're drawn into her. Other times she'll shut that off, and is very cold, very cool and I don't blame her because I don't give her as much time as I should – a lot of company members feel I don't give them enough time. She definitely wants a part of me.

'Paula listens. People tend to forget her acute powers of hearing and observation. Recently in a piece she wrote the word "yew". Jan corrected it to "you" and Paula was adamant she meant yew. She knew it was a tree with mystical powers. How could she know that? The Rees family didn't, and I certainly didn't know the yew tree had these associations. She assimilates information.'

Paula had written:

'Mary a favourite, a rare someone, fallen from a yew, my message to Mary is go see feel my fast great seed of life far we must go to take the story so far.'

'The crime,' says Mary, 'from society's point of

view, is all this stimulation and all this acknow-ledgement should have happened from the time Paula was born. Instead society puts people to one side, says they have no quality of life and treats them like inanimate objects.

'Her peers look after Paula. As a team they're totally self-sufficient, they deal with Paula's needs as they deal with each other's needs, at Chicken Shed, out together at schools. There is no need for Jan or Eddie to take care of her.

'They would like her to have a life of her own, and that *is* difficult for her peers to take on because of the practicalities. It's getting the wheelchair into the car, it's having to have a car which will take the wheel-chair. It's easy to say, "Surely they could organise that" and point the finger, but these are just young kids, and they're taking on a lot more than most kids of their age do. But Paula has the opportunity now, she works with the team and that's the beginning of a social scene. Naturally when she goes to lunch, she's with them. Paula should have gone to school with them and it would be easy.'

I asked one of Paula's teammates and friends if she thought Paula's gift came as a result of all those years of frustration, her lips metaphorically sealed. Had she been normal, would she still have had her bright creative talent?

Fiona thought about this. 'She would still have been the same Paula, with the same gift, but she might not have found it.'

Paul Morrall was taking a Chicken Shed session in

one of the local schools. During the class he taught the children to sing 'I Wish I Could Talk' by Paula. And he talked about her and her life.

At the end of the class, two little girls came up to Paul. 'Please, Sir, is that lady real, or is she just a story?'

'She's real, all right,' he said. 'Next week I'll bring her along, and you can see for yourself.'

CHAPTER 19

Life makes us tame

Life makes us tame
Ask what is sane
See what remains
Answers the same

Behind the closed door of the freshly painted blue and yellow room which is Paula's, overlooking the garden, Kerri and Ian were describing for me the childhood they had shared. Outside, the youngest members of the family – Kerri's son Connor and Ian's son Kyle – played noisily. Kyle, not yet old enough for school, lives mostly with Jan and Eddie since Ian and his partner split up in the summer of 1996.

In the living room, Jan, her hair encased in a plastic bag processing the highlights Kerri had applied earlier, the telephone handset clamped to her ear, maintained a series of conversations while keeping an ear open for possible demands from the children. Eddie had taken Adam to a rehearsal (he plays drums and sings with Chicken Shed's junior jazz band). In the middle of the room sat Paula in her chair, silently looking around, fluttering hands. You get the feeling that the tempo of life here has never changed, barring small details.

As small children Ian and Kerri took for granted the lifestyle determined for them by Paula being 'the way she was'. The realisation that Paula's frailty wasn't just that she couldn't walk but was life-threatening came later.

'We were used to illness and hospital,' explained Kerri. 'She used to go into hospital so often, problems like she couldn't feed or she'd get a really bad cold and had to be hospitalised, it went without saying.

'It didn't really hit me that she could actually die until she had the scoliosis operation. I couldn't talk about it at home, I wasn't able to. That was when I went a bit wild, stayed away from home where I could be by myself. Or went to clubs – I wanted to go out and enjoy myself. It was a totally self-centred thing. I just wanted to do what I wanted to do and that was it. I think about the way I behaved at that time, it added to their troubles. They must have been worried sick.'

Ian said: 'You were a rebel weren't you?'

'I don't think I would have done what I did in normal circumstances.'

Working behind the bar at the Kit Kat Club in Bayswater she found the only person in whom she was able to confide her fears about Paula. It was an eccentric watering hole – she served only coffee and cans of Coke; if they wished, members were permitted to bring in their own alcohol. The owner was a former social worker who had worked with the miners during the 1984–85 strike, and putting on a benefit for them had led to him setting up the club. 'Because he was older than me (he celebrated his twenty-ninth birthday several years running, as I recall) and because we worked alongside each other, conversation just happened. I was able to tell him how scared I was for Paula and us. It was a relief of sorts.'

Ian was younger when he realised that Paula was not only 'different', but she was also very ill. 'I understood but I didn't want to understand. I tried to put it out of my mind.

'I had problems of my own. School was a problem, I was dyslexic, every day was a problem. At the time of the scoliosis, my school problems were like a nightmare, constant trouble with the teachers, Kerri had left home, I had so much on my plate I was able to blot out thinking about how ill Paula was, at least some of the time.'

Did the never-ending discussion about Paula, how was her day, was she sleeping well, eating, was she in pain, was she happy or moody, make him yearn to be the centre of their attention?

'I didn't want them to ask about my day, I didn't want to talk about it.'

And yet their parents always managed to give them the time they needed. 'Not once,' said Kerri, 'have I ever felt Mum and Dad didn't have time for me or Ian. They always had time, fitted it in some-how, I don't know how they did it. Everything we did was family. I never felt things were rushed because they had so much to do.'

As parents themselves now they can identify with Jan and Eddie.

'They were so young,' said Kerri. Ian added: 'It takes someone special to do what they did, and on top of that I think of all the problems they had with me at school.'

The family closeness is the foundation of their lives. Kerri: 'I can talk to Mum and Dad about absolutely everything. I look at other families, a friend will have a problem and I'll say, "Why don't you speak to your parents about it?", and it just wouldn't occur to them. Emotionally if I'm hurt or upset about something, and I can't talk to Mark [her husband] about it, I ask Mum or Dad. Perhaps I rely on them too much. Ian doesn't, he locks everything in.'

Ian: 'My parents always know if I have a problem, they can hear it in my voice.'

Kerri: 'I never felt, "If I do this they won't love me any more." I always felt secure.'

Both knew their parents to be fair and reasonable. Anger and being cross didn't last, except when Jan was on the warpath against some bureaucratic injustice.

Kerri: 'Perhaps if you have a child like Paula, you have to be laidback about most things – they had such huge problems to worry about, little problems aren't worth bothering with.'

Eddie 'is one of those quiet people you can push a long way, then suddenly he'll lose it,' Ian explained, referring in particular to an occasion when he, Ian, took himself off for a haircut and came home with a Mohican tuft. Eddie, whose fury was directed at the perpetrator, marched his pubescent son straight back to the barber's shop and demanded the only solution: a clean, full-head shave.

The episode passed into the catalogue of family jokes, and still brings a laugh: Punk to skinhead in one day!

214

They were not aware of the family's financial struggle (on holiday they were always allowed an ice cream every day); on the other hand it came naturally to them not to pitch their hopes too high and ask for 'ridiculous' things.

When friends were given smart new bicycles Eddie had an answer. 'Dad would turn that around,' said Ian. 'He'd buy an old bike [they were always expert at finding bargains, even in pre-car-boot days] and make it look as good or better than the new ones in the shop. "It's custom made, son, it's better," he'd say, and I could see he was right.

'I did eventually get a new bike. I asked for one one Christmas, and three Christmases later I got it.'

Owning a bicycle was part of the 'street cred' in their district. When Jan won £300 at bingo on the eve of Kerri's tenth birthday, Kerri had her first new bike as a birthday present, a purple Tomahawk. It replaced the treasured bicycle passed on by her aunt, so old it had solid tyres. Once when it was stolen the thief subsequently returned it, dumping it overnight on the path outside the front door.

Many family anecdotes are rooted in being hard up. Once on holiday, Ian was given the total contents of Jan's purse, scraped together to buy ham for tea. He came back from the shop having spent the lot on a jar of jam ('they didn't have no ham') and wearing a *Planet of the Apes* mask which he had coveted desperately since catching sight of it in the campsite shop. 'I wanted that mask so badly.' Mention holiday and it brings to Ian's mind his memory of Eddie 'on the rocks in Wales, wearing his Pepsi

T-shirt, long hair, looking so young.'

When Kerri was around thirteen, she became aware that her friends 'could go out and buy loads of clothes', which she envied. 'But it taught me to be a bit cleverer, you have to shop around. Even if I've got a hundred pounds I want bargains for that. I shop at Oxfam, I make my own, I go to car-boot sales. There is no way I would pay £40 for trainers, even if I was rich. I suppose if I won the lottery I'd like to go out and buy clothes with designer labels; right now I look at anyone wearing a £60 shirt and it looks exactly the same as one for £2.99 in the market.' Ian too hankered after trainers, jeans and football shirts but they were out of his league and there was no big brother handing them down. 'And I always wanted a football kit but I never got one. It was a lot of money, it wasn't necessary so it wasn't on.' Friends had after-school jobs to earn pocket money but Jan put her foot down, reminding him he had enough trouble getting up for school without trying to fit in a paper round.

Kerri remembers sharing a room with Paula, who used to scratch the polystyrene tiles on the wall and grind her teeth which kept her sister awake for many hours. 'Even now when she starts doing that it drives me mad. You couldn't stop Paula doing anything.'

Ian said: 'Sometimes when I was a kid I used to sleep downstairs with my Dad, and Paula used to sleep in her special room downstairs, and I had this fantasy that in the night she'd get up and walk around and talk.

'If anyone ever asked, "What would you wish for if you had the chance?", my wish was always that Paula would talk. Once I heard her say "Ian" but I didn't tell anyone. Who would have believed me? Now I'm not sure if I believe it myself.'

They know instinctively how Paula is feeling at a given time. Ian says he can walk into a room 'and get the vibes that Paula is annoyed with me, her head goes back and her legs kick a little.'

Paula rarely cries. She did, desperately, when their grandmother died; hurtful behaviour by a friend, lack of support or discovering that someone she trusts turns out not to believe in her can make her weep. 'She's quite a toughie,' said Kerri, 'and quite unforgiving. Once she has shut someone out they do not get a second chance, she can't afford to give second chances I suppose.

'I argue with her a lot and she knows how to wind me up. Once she said, "I can get someone to do your job at half the price." [Kerri is employed as her part-time carer.] "Really? Find someone then," I replied, and she quickly responded, "Only joking." We often have little spats. The first time she said to me, "You've got the sack," I was really upset. Now I ignore her.'

Each day Kerri selects what Paula is to wear – up to a point. If she is going somewhere special, Paula specifies her outfit, hair, make-up, jewellery. They shop together. Paula is passionately clothes conscious, knows her style, is fussily selective going through the rails and having outfits held up to her face for inspection in front of the full-length mirror.

Any trying on has to be done at home. Once she hated the colour red, now she loves it; she adores the unconventional, the arty, the way-out.

When they disagreed over a multi-coloured Naf Naf jumpsuit (orange, yellow, blue, green – brilliant neon colours like an overgrown BabyGro) Paula insisted on buying it and wore it flamboyantly. Kerri calls her a prima donna. 'She has to go to every shop before she will make up her mind.' She likes change, her clothes have a modest wardrobe life before they are passed on to friends' children.

In the shoe shop every single pair has to come out. Because she is a size 11 she's classed as having a child's foot, but she doesn't want to dress as a child, so searching for shoes is an ongoing process. At any given time she is likely to have twenty-five pairs of shoes and boots – many of them hand made – in her shoe box. When they are passed on to new owners, they have never touched the ground.

Ian and Kerri grew up with instincts finely tuned to any slur, inadvertent or intended. 'Children in the park who didn't know us well might make remarks about "that spastic". You'd either lose your temper and thump them or walk off in silence, huffy,' said Kerri. 'A few people at school took the mickey out of Paula, trying to wind me up,' commented Ian. 'It never really bothered me but if it did, I used to hit them and it seemed to work. I didn't want to know people like that.'

They agree they were choosy, and believe it taught them to judge character. Friends who knew them well, including neighbourhood children

(Paula was part of the community), were acceptable and reliable. Others had to be seen to be trusted. Bring the wrong person home and the result could be embarrassing, not because Paula was an embarrassment but in case the visitor upset Paula or Jan. You had to be sure of your friends before you invited them through the door.

Kerri and Ian are warm and caring. Ian seems older than his years. 'I always felt older than I was. I always thought I had to act older than I was because of the Paula situation, and needing to be aware of the burden Mum and Dad carried.'

He had a brief period of 'going a bit wild, like Kerri did' after he left school, staying out all night in other people's houses and clubs. 'For my fifteenth birthday I went out and that was the first time I was offered Ecstasy, that was my era (I was nine when Ecstasy first came out). And I got hooked on that, the music and the vibes. Ecstasy was imported from America, the tablets were made in a factory not somebody's house, each tablet cost £25 then, now they're cheap and made from dangerous mixes and that's why people are dropping down. To go out and sit and listen to the music, dance, drop one [tablet], you wouldn't do it at home, it's part of a party scene.

'Everyone was on something when I was in my teens, my social life was drug orientated. Back then your parents would flip if they thought you were smoking pot, our parents used to think if you burned a joss stick you were on drugs – if you smoked pot you were a lost cause. Today it's accepted by most parents; it is a part of society that there are different levels of drugs, not all threatening.'

Ian concluded: 'I don't regret that I did that.'

Kerri: 'I don't regret the drugs, but I wouldn't want my child to do it. I'd have a fit if I thought he was going out doing half the things I did. I just grew out of it. I met Mark and wasn't interested in going out any more, and lost touch with that scene.'

Ian: 'Like been there, done that . . . lack of funds has something to do with it.'

Kerri: 'Drugs are socially addictive. You felt you couldn't go out and stay awake all night unless you took something. Ecstasy wasn't around then . . . now there's Ecstasy and LSD. I wouldn't take anything like that.'

'It's having a child,' remarked Ian. 'You've got to think about the long term effects as well. You want to be around as long as you can, don't you, when you've got a kid.'

'Suppose you were drunk, suppose you took a tablet and you were tripping and somebody phoned up and said your child's been rushed to hospital,' said Kerri. 'That's got to be a major nightmare. I'm worried if I go out and get drunk now.

'I was going to Wales on a riding holiday, and before I booked I checked how much it would cost if Connor needed me and I had to fly back in an emergency! Life moves on. I have friends who are forty, still living as they did fifteen years ago, in one room, going out to clubs and pubs, having nothing of substance.'

Ian's phase of being a 'bit wild' had ended when he met Nicky. Their four-year relationship produced

Kyle. The birth was traumatic and scary, there were numerous complications which resulted in a Caesarian delivery. Jan sat throughout at the hospital; Eddie went home to be with Paula during the long wait. In the kitchen he broke down and cried. 'Dad thought it was happening all over again, that this was how Paula was born, could it be the same for his grandchild? He didn't want this for me, he knew what he had been through.'

In the event Kyle was born a healthy, robust child, and Ian is working hard to build up his business as a carpet fitter, intent on moving out of the high-rise block and to somewhere with a garden where the children (ideally, he would like three more) can play.

Not Kerri. For her one is enough. 'My mum was with me throughout the birth. I couldn't have done it without her beside me. As it was I thought I was going to die, I think I told her so . . . I think I told her I wanted to die.'

How do they explain Paula to their children? Accepting doesn't mean there doesn't have to be an explanation, surely?

Ian: 'I've told Kyle that Paula's got wheels for legs. He understands that.'

Kerri: 'I remember saying to Connor that Paula can't walk, or talk, but she understands everything that's said. That's the only explanation needed, he's never queried it.

'Often children come up and ask what's wrong with her. I've overheard parents tell a child, "She's not very well", and thought it a ridiculous answer. I

221

tell them, "She can't walk, she can't speak, but she hears everything you say. It's just that her legs and her arms don't work." And they understand that. I'd rather adults came up and asked instead of looking sideways, muttering and appearing embarrassed.'

They live with the anxiety of Paula's health. She suffers constant pain in her neck above the fusion scar, her legs are becoming more twisted, and another operation has been ruled out. Kerri is frustrated that regular physiotherapy from a qualified physiotherapist is simply not available; at best all they can expect is an occasional visit and suggested guidance. 'Not being trained, you don't know how far you can go, there is a fear of causing damage. It isn't even as if she can describe how it feels.'

It is a curious dichotomy: Paula, so physically helpless yet at the same time so strong in talent and personality that they are in awe of her achievements. Neither understands Paula's gifts, especially her ability to write in the 'voice' of Shakespeare (as she did for *A Midsummer Night's Dream*) having never read or seen Shakespeare performed, in common with the rest of the family. Not directly involved in the work of Chicken Shed (Kerri occasionally helps with make-up; their children are beginning to join in), they are nevertheless feeling its influence, and Ian watches Shakespeare on video with total enjoyment.

Could they imagine life without Paula? 'I can't even contemplate it,' said Kerri. 'I'm more concerned with what would it be like if there is no Mum and Dad. They're young but they've had such hard lives, they do so much. Dad is darting about all the time, he is under so much pressure, so much stress which he never talks about. They never had much money, and Dad always worked so hard. I look at their lives and feel really sorry for them, and when does it end for them?'

Ian always worried about his parents and has never stopped worrying about them. 'I can remember Mum sitting down sometimes when we were young and saying, "I just can't handle it no more." She'd be crying, it was all getting on top of her.' But alongside those memories are the positive ones, Jan's going out to work in the evenings being the reason Eddie would put the record player on and teach them to waltz.

'In some ways,' said Ian, 'I think we had a better childhood than many others.'

'Totally,' agreed Kerri. 'I wouldn't change my childhood, not for my sake or Paula's.'

'If we could change anything,' added Ian, 'it would be for Paula to enjoy our childhood as we did. Paula missed out.'

'Not on everything,' said Kerri. But that triggers another image. 'I would be at a club, dancing, and in the middle of enjoying myself I'd suddenly think of Paula, and wondered what it felt like not being able to dance.

'When I got married, that was the worst time, thinking about Paula, "She can never have this."

'People said, "Aren't you nice, having your sister as bridesmaid." Everyone's sister is a bridesmaid, surely? I wanted it to be important for her, as it was for me. She'll never have a wedding day.

'And then I had Connor, and I was so happy, except that that made me think of Paula and feel truly sorry for her.

'I try not to think about the future. I've spoken to Mum and Dad about this – if anything happened to them, or they got to an age when they couldn't cope, then Paula would live with me, that's understood. Ian knows that.'

Ian agrees that this makes sense; after all he is just a brother, sisters are closer. But Kerri knows that both her brothers can be depended upon.

Chapter 20

For Dom Placid, my priest

As long as you love
As long as you give
As long as you are free
As long as you live for the good
So life will be

We were drinking tea in Jan's front room. Paula
had been taken out of her chair to rest her back; she
was lying face down on the carpet. She was smiling
and making her mewing noises. Eddie had just
pulled up her vest to show me her operation scars, a
series of lines graphically following the surgeon's
work. She weighs three and a half stone ('and half of
that is metal – if we ever took you abroad you'd set
off all those alarm bells going through security,' says
Jan). Paula likes to chew the end of her plait and
has been warned she'll end up with fur balls, like a
cat. When Adam comes in from school, he kneels
down and kisses her, without a word spoken.

Jan says that Father Dom Placid, the priest at
Vita et Pax, calls Paula the closest thing to an angel
he has ever seen, and makes her sit in the front pew
when she goes to church.

'She affects people in so many ways,' says Jan.
'The whole of my life, all the pain and everything
that has happened, I'd go through it again for what
Paula has achieved. Even if she hadn't been a
poet . . . all my children are beautiful, but Paula is
radiant. She never asks for anything from us,
except sometimes a cuddle and a kiss. I am not a

religious person, but if I thought there was something special which came from God, then it is Paula. Paula is the closest thing I can imagine to a religious experience. I don't need her to answer me, I don't need her to say yes.

'I want people to recognise her creativity. What she has gone through to achieve what she has achieved must come into your story, but Paula's story is a positive one – even if just one mum out there reads about Paula, she's just had a child, she believes her child's future is hopeless and she reads about Paula and is able to feel there's some hope.'

Kerri had taken Paula out, lifting her effortlessly in her arms as you would cradle a baby or a gangling puppy, Paula's head flopping back not with tension but in bliss.

'I used to ask myself why her, why me? When I first knew about Paula, I believed she would improve. I would look at other children at the centre and think, "Well, of course she won't be as bad as that." I always thought she would eventually walk, and certainly talk, that we would get there somehow, eventually, but there comes a time when you know that she isn't going to do those things, that she can never hope for a normal healthy life. But that realisation doesn't happen overnight, it is gradual, and gradually I stopped hoping and learned to accept that there was no miracle, there wasn't even a chance of a little improvement around the corner.

'When she eventually left school, and there was nowhere else for her, I felt this dreadful sense of failure. Why hadn't I done more? If I had been more intelligent, better educated I could have helped her in so many ways. I'd never done enough. Was there something in the *system* which had I known about it, had access to it, I could have used for Paula? The more her intelligence was revealed, the more her talent and gift for words, the worse it was to contemplate what it must have been like all those years for Paula, locked in, unable to reach out.

'Then I started to meet people at Chicken Shed, and saw what other parents had achieved, how they knew the ropes because they were bright and educated and not afraid to speak up. I used to be so trusting, always assume that *they* know best. I'm not like that any more, I've learned to confront issues. And I refuse to let myself get upset unless it's over something I have to fight over. Ignorant remarks, insensitive actions . . . I just walk away, it's their loss if they can't see reality.'

Jan is sensitive, possibly oversensitive, to any slight. An official filling out a form asks, 'And what centre does she attend, Mrs Rees?' 'She doesn't attend a *centre*, she's a poet; she is artist in residence at Chicken Shed Theatre Company. If you don't mind!'

Jan goes on. 'No matter how much she achieves, she still cannot wash away the surface Paula which people see, and by which they label her.

'It's as if she is labelled for ever. We're labelled. I'm labelled a fat person.

'My son's French teacher at school called three boys out to the front of the class, in order to demonstrate the use of adjectives. Three boys, one tall, one short, one fat.

229

' "Don't take this personally," said the teacher, and invited the class to find words to distinguish the boys' physical characteristics. My Adam was the fat boy. He felt humiliated. He would have liked to have been called to the front for some other reason, like his smile or his shiny hair. It didn't have to be because he was fat.

' "Do I look fat in this jacket, Mum?" he asked next day. And now, often, "Will I be slimmer when I grow up?"

'It is one thing when remarks are made in ignorance, but another thing when insensitive remarks are meted out by professionals. Surely even if they don't *know* better, they've been trained.'

Even small things can be potentially hurtful to Jan. It was by way of being a spectacular feather in Chicken Shed's cap when, after catching their show at the Hard Rock Café in Piccadilly, music promoter Andrew Miller invited the company to give a concert on the occasion of his and showbiz lawyer Willi Robertson receiving their Silver Cleft awards from the British Music Industry. This was serious prestige – as was the event, dinner at the Grosvenor House Hotel, Park Lane. But Paula wasn't able to use the stairs and had to go down to the ballroom, where the ceremony was being held, in the kitchen lift. Afterwards everyone adjourned upstairs to the balcony to mingle with the performers and say their goodbyes, and Paula had to wait downstairs because now the kitchen was too busy to let her through. Catherine Zeta Jones and her favourite, Meatloaf, were there, upstairs, talking to departing Chicken Shedders.

Jan became anxious for Paula's sake, but Mary had already begun to wend her way downstairs, leading assorted celebrities including Meatloaf and Catherine Zeta Jones.

Meatloaf sat down next to Paula. 'I feel really proud meeting you, Paula,' he said.

Jan said: 'She says yes by lifting her eyebrows.'

'Yes,' he said. 'I know that.'

He kissed her, and sat holding her hand and kissing it from time to time. 'I was thinking that I could do with one of those kisses,' says Jan. He said how moving he found her lyrics. Paula loved him straight away. However, she was decidedly cool towards one well-known performer who beckoned photographers – she was not prepared to be just a photo-opportunity.

Meatloaf said he would like her to write a song for him, which she did, and sent the tape. But she heard nothing.

'She would have liked an acknowledgement, even if it was to say he thought it a load of rubbish. It isn't as if he doesn't have legions of people to write letters for him. However, next day his manager telephoned Chicken Shed to invite them to perform, with him, on stage at Wembley, singing and dancing to Paula's song "Have a Heart at Christmas".'

They went along for rehearsals. 'He sat next to me,' says Jan. ' "Hi," ' he said, so he certainly remembered me. He was sweet and gentle to Paula, and crouched down beside her to speak to her at her level. Several days later she wrote that when he crouched down beside her, he whispered, "Feel free, Paula."

'On the night of the Wembley performance, he talked on stage about Chicken Shed, and that he knew what it felt like, not to have people believe in you.

'I found him a genuine, lovely man. He didn't seek publicity from it. His wife was lovely, too. I just wonder if somebody in his organisation just popped the tape in a drawer and never passed it on to him.'

There was a postscript. Visiting the family caravan several months later, the Reeses met up with a family of four brothers, friends they jokingly call The Andrews Sisters because Andrews is their surname. The boys told how they had managed to get tickets to see their idol, Meatloaf, at Wembley. And who comes on stage? Little Paula in her wheelchair. By the end of the song everyone was crying with emotion and the boys went home thinking, 'All our life we've wanted to meet Meatloaf. We can't manage it. Guess who does!'

Paula's emergence into the outside world, and then becoming something of a celebrity, required an update in the Rees's transport arrangements. The van had to go: it performed only after you started the engine and then engaged in a gymnastic display; during one of these sessions Jan managed to run over her own leg, which led to her suffering a severe bout of depression, not to mention the fracture. But they needed the cash for its replacement.

They were receiving £120 a month in mobility allowance. By giving this up for five years, and applying for a 'motorbility' allowance, they were allocated money towards the cost of a van, although the grant effectively took sixteen months to arrive.

Paula met the Princess of Wales during one of Diana's visits to Chicken Shed, and as a result had written a poem especially for her, which was duly acknowledged:

Dearest Paula,
    Thank you so much for your beautiful poem. Having been lucky enough to meet you I'm all the more touched that you should have taken the trouble to send me such wise and thoughtful words. Through your writing, and in many other ways, I hope you will always be able to let others share in your own strength.
    Lots of love
    from
    Diana x

It was Jan's turn to meet Princess Diana when they were invited to a garden party.

'Sandy Gonzalez [one of the original Chicken Shed mothers] organised a Daimler and sent it around the day before to check that Paula's chair would fit into it, and it did. "We've got to go in style," she said. I bought a black silk skirt and top, with a black and white spotted blouse to go over, open because otherwise it was too tight.

'For about a fortnight she was rehearsing me in what to say. She was very precise. "When she comes to meet you, you hold out your hand and you say, 'Pleased to meet you, ma'am.'" I kept practising.

233

This became an obsession with Sandy. "Don't forget, Janet. No swearing or that." We knew Princess Diana was going to speak to us. Paula had written a poem for her and she had written to thank her for it.

'Anyway, so she came along the line and stopped to talk to Paula. Then Sandy said, "And this is Paula's mum," and Princess Diana said, "Hello, Mrs Rees," and I said, "Hello luv, nice to see you." I just forgot myself – I thought Sandy was going to explode.

'And Princess Diana said: "You must be so proud of Paula, she's such a star." '

Finis

As nature takes time

As nature takes time
And life takes love
As good takes bad

And hope takes fear
So we can give
And so we can live

And now we see
What love can do
Life gives us the need

To find the strength
And learn to fight
For all the truth

As questions are asked
And answers are given
Still the story stays the same

As love takes love
And hate takes hate
A good story is happy ever after